Praying to Know Him

"PRAYING FROM MY SOUL"

Denise P. Ford

Praying To Know Him: Praying From My Soul

Foreword

I felt blessed and truly honored as I was given this manuscript to read. I was truly uplifted and encouraged by the anointing that exuded from every chapter. *Praying to know Him: Praying from my soul* gives an astounding insight into understanding the power of prayer. It also gives additional meaning into how a person starts to commit themselves toward building a personal relationship with Christ through prayer. Each chapter expounds upon the experiences, facts, and uncommon situations that a person must endure in order to ultimately find salvation and peace in Christ.

Praying to Know Him is very concise when emphasizing that this can only be obtained when you know Christ through heartfelt prayers. Each page provides you with spiritual nuggets and discourse which makes a person think, ponder, and pray. I consider this book to be a blueprint or manual for someone who desires to build a successful and relevant prayer life regardless of their situation. *Praying to Know Him* has all the attributes of a celestial journey that inclines our hearts and minds to finally accept and remain connected to Christ through prayer. After reading this writing, I understand further the statement "God looks at the Heart" (1 Samuel 16:7).

Blessings and peace as you turn each page to understand the many blessings that are revealed.

Elder Thomas E. Walker
MACM, Liberty Baptist Theological Seminary
Founder and Senior Minister of Reflections of Grace Outreach Ministries, Inc.
Author of *My Steps Have Already Been Ordered*

Dedication

I dedicate this work in loving memory to my grandparents, the late Bishop Ceasar A. Ford and Betty B. Ford. You were true farmers and fishers of men. There is a part of who you were that lives on inside of me, your legacy of hard work and spirit of sowing. The harvest will be plenty as the seeds fall on good ground.

Contents

Introduction

$\mathcal{S}$ometimes, we are thrust on a path that may take us away from our family, friends, comfort zone, or environment. It may feel as though we've been punished, abandoned, or stricken by a series of unfortunate events; but when God is behind the scenes there is a divine work that he is preparing us for.

When we find ourselves in desperate situations or in trouble, where else is there to turn for refuge from the madness that we face? Our ultimate help is to call on God; He is faithful and sincere about those who call upon Him. Prayer has been the essential foundation of connecting us to the answers that are found in God. Many of us have been taught to kneel and pray as children before going to bed, to say grace before eating our meals, or while giving thanks and revering God. As we continue to be grateful we have learned to turn to our faith.

Since we cannot see God as we desire to, we are forced to pray and are left with the hope that He hears us. The world is vast with many cultures, religions, and people from all nations with different backgrounds. God is omnipotent, omnipresent, and omniscient. We are made in the image of God and He desires for us to love and worship Him. He is the source that provides to us the fundamentals to live and to use our God given abilities and free will to carry out our life's assignments. However, the mission is critical, but prayer is the ultimate tool and resource for communicating and receiving the instructions that one needs to succeed.

It would be very difficult to prepare for war and expect to win the battle without knowledge, proper training, and the tools to fight. When we enter war, we cannot see everything that the enemy is doing, what devices are being utilized, and how many soldiers are fighting against us. Therefore, we must turn to prayer and consult with God in order to get the victory. It does not matter how much information that we may think or feel we know, because there are forces of good and evil going to battle in the spirit realm along with us.

As we learn to hold on to our hope and faith, there is a reason why change is inevitable. God is putting together all of the pieces to the puzzle in our lives. He is the Master Potter and we are the jars of clay, as He continues to form us into His masterpiece. Our souls are being purged of the old things while He is bringing us forth as pure gold, to offer us an abundant life in knowing him.

When we worship and confess our faith in God, His presence draws near to our hearts. The entire universe is His and He desires to have every living being in unity worshipping Him. His glory is indescribable and the angels know how to truly worship Him. We cannot fathom what it really means to surrender when our minds are so full of earthly distractions. We must continue to surrender our will to God daily, because He's on our side.

As we bow down to pray, let us come boldly to the throne of grace and make it personal and let our praise be heard for every petition, victory, favor, blessing, suffering, and cry that touches heaven. We must not stop there because Jesus wants an intimate relationship and longs for our hearts to delight in knowing Him. The moment that we surrender to God's Spirit, His blessings will fall down on us. He will continue to guide our hearts because His intimacy and love for us means more to Him than we could ever know.

CHAPTER I

The Prayer Box – Natural Sins

There are so many people secretly battling with the agony of going through trials, tests, surgeries, decisions about a loved one on life support, fear of dying, finding shelter, facing eviction, hunger, domestic and sexual assault, joblessness, lack of money to buy medicine, demonic attacks, un-forgiveness, dementia, terminal illness, court battles, and the list goes on. It can be overwhelming just hearing about any of these circumstances that have stricken someone's life. My heart is beating rapidly just imagining how I would cope through any of these issues. It is indeed a divine work that must be given to God above.

We get so wrapped up into our own troubles, by whining and complaining, without even knowing how badly our neighbor could be suffering and on the brink of losing their mind or life. I am guilty of not being consciously aware of my neighbor's woes, or sometimes asking if everything is alright. We could help someone if we desired to, even if we don't have money or material things to give, or by saying a prayer, touching, and agreeing for God to help those who are in need and to bless each prayer box that has been designated at the church. There is someone who wants to die because they have lost hope. The single mother in the grocery store that walked out because she didn't have enough money to pay for her child's medicine maybe contemplating suicide.

Sometimes life can beat you down to the point that you may give up trying. If only we knew how much worse someone else had it, we'd be more joyful, hopeful, and grateful not to complain about our own problems. We would be able to find more things to be optimistic about rather than harboring the petty things that really don't make a big difference. As we think about how good God is in spite of the problems we face, there is still purpose in everything that we go through. God's word is working in our lives every day to prove that it is infallible and we can put our trust in Him. There is no other source or answer to life's dilemmas, but to turn to God in prayer.

I believe that the Lord connects those who pray to Him with others who believe in the power of His love and mercy. Sometimes, we may not have the answer in front of us, but by having the heart to serve the Lord, He will reveal the answer to us. There are so many prayers that are being sent to God daily, asking for things that are available to us on earth. When we intercede in prayer for a need to be met, we are preparing our minds and hearts to be used for His will and glory. We will distinctly know it's the Lord leading and instructing us to perform these tasks, miracles, and assignments. People who doubt if God can help them are sometimes unable to recognize when their blessing has arrived. We must encourage hope and share our faith in God, no matter what we may be facing.

There is suffering and pain that we cannot see with our physical eyes. The woes are buried deep within the crevices of the soul. Sometimes it's hard to know the best words to say that will lift someone's spirit or that can touch the heart of the wounded. I've learned to pray for the person anyway, because it's important that heaven hears my prayer. We are in a spiritual war and when a soldier is down, it's the next soldier's responsibility to cover the wounded soldier. As I pray for others to be healed and for God's will to be done in their lives, I ask God to help me pass my tests. I want my life to be used for His glory and to be a vessel that He can use. There is so much work to be done as a soldier prepares for war.

There are thousands of prayer boxes holding the hope, tears, intricate concerns, fears, beliefs, doubts, anger, disappointments, faith, and final requests of the souls that are in need and requests by intercessors standing in the gap.

There is no amount of money that can move heaven when it comes to asking and needing the Lord to answer a prayer. It seems fair because there are two spheres that exist: heaven and earth. The earth is governed by the laws of the land, power, money, and political influence. The human race has learned that there are those who have and the have-nots. It's the way of life, and which side you fall depends on whether you will have adequate resources, opportunities, and other options to live a better life.

The heavenly realm is where your prayers are sent when earth cannot handle its requests. There are infinite resources and eternal happiness within our reach. He doesn't want us to have money, good credit, and a spotless life to come to Him. Jesus died for our sins and He offers salvation and eternal life for those who believe and accept that He is the Son of God. If you believe in Jesus, you must surrender your life and will to God.

Sometimes the road in life can seem lonely and endless. When we come to the end of a matter and cannot do anything else about it, now is the time to give it to God and allow His will to be done. If you are ever down and need someone to talk to, you can call on the name of Jesus. When you pray to our Lord and savior, feel free to express whatever you feel. He is always there to listen and draw near. It doesn't matter about the situation you're in or what you've done, the Lord is waiting. When we start a relationship with Jesus through prayer, he moves.

It is through our faith and not with our human understanding that we believe in Christ Jesus. He is a Spirit whom we worship in Spirit and truth! We are born into this world without any knowledge that we have trespassed against God by Adam's disobedience to God and his fall to sin in the Garden of Eden. His sinful nature was passed down to us the human race. It was through God's mercy to not destroy us and punish us for offending Him by breaking fellowship with Him and doing things contrary to His will.

As we study the scriptures we learn in the book of John and Hebrews why God gave His only begotten Son Jesus to the world. He is our Savior, and Lord and High Priest whom reconciled us back to God the Father. He forgave our sins and made propitiation for the sins of the people. Jesus was formed in the flesh by God and filled with God's Spirit as He came to show us love, and to offer us forgiveness for our sins and to save us by giving us salvation and everlasting life.

He knew us before we were placed into our mother's womb. He knows everything about us and how we feel and the things we are faced with. If you don't know where to go or how to live a fulfilling life, will you take the time out to accept Jesus Christ and your gift of salvation? The next step would be baptism and building a relationship with Jesus through the Holy Bible and prayer.

If you choose Christ, He will turn your life around and fill you with peace, love, and joy. In addition, to your gift of salvation you will have eternal life. I'm a living witness that you don't have to understand everything to accept his gift and grace, because in time it will all come together. Remember that the troubles in your life will not completely go away, but He will give you the strength and grace and the Holy Spirit to endure it. When you accept Him, the angels in heaven sing praises and they rain down blessings to show His glory!

I never pondered why there was a prayer box placed at church, until I realized how desperately I needed a prayer answered. I felt too ashamed to share my personal matters, because of the pain and suffering that I've experienced. I could only relate to how miserable it felt walking around with constant worry from day to day and not having no one to confide in or knowing where I could go for refuge and to leave my burdens. Suddenly, I thought that I could write down my prayer requests and put it into the church's prayer box without anyone knowing. Have you ever needed a prayer answered when you could do nothing else about your situation?

The prayer box is designated for God to manifest His will and power in the lives of the souls that truly love Him. His love is real and divine. It matters to God that we seek Him because our true peace is in knowing Him. Sometimes, we may feel pushed or forced to attend church and aren't ready to follow others there, yet. The Lord knows how to get our attention, and when the time comes, all we need to do is surrender.

I remember a time in my life when I was burdened down with marital problems, work issues, and fears about my future; I couldn't stop worrying nor turn my brain off from thinking negative thoughts. I made a lot of bad choices and mistakes; I didn't feel worthy of knowing whether God heard my prayers. It was exhausting and overwhelming to my soul. I did pray for myself but I wanted someone else who was stronger to pray with me, because I was weak and weary. The enemy had me captive inside of his web of lies. Every little thing that I thought was going to happen badly somehow didn't go quite as bad, so I kept on praying and reading the Bible for answers and strength. I didn't know at the time that the battle was on the inside of me and being unequally yoked did cause the majority of the attacks I suffered.

The attacks went on for some time, then I developed anxiety attacks and my health started going downhill. My legs and hands were tingling and I couldn't breathe without grasping for air. I was horrified; the more that I worried, the worse my condition got. I remember walking one day and my legs gave out on me, and that was when I panicked. I continued to cry out to the Lord and pray as much as I knew how to. I went to several doctors to have more tests done. As I searched for answers to why my health was declining, I moved forward by faith hoping that God would send me to the right physician. I received some spiritual advice from one of my sisters-in-law. She told me to read the Psalms 23 chapter and anoint my body from head to toe with Virgin Olive Oil and pray healing over myself. I immediately followed her instructions and that's when I found true relief in waiting patiently for God to turn my situation around for the better.

Eventually, I was diagnosed with chronic anxiety and stress. One of my doctor's suggested that I may have to divorce my husband because I confided in him about the intimate issues that I was having and I didn't realize that I had reached my limit of what I couldn't control nor was I able to cope anymore in concealing the pain. I knew that I was in trouble and my health was scaring me enough to make changes in my life that would shape my destiny.

As I prayed for God to deliver me the walls started falling down all around me. I spent time alone going for walks around a nature trail where there was a scenic route and lake. I was searching for God to speak to me and to lift these burdens off of me. It's amazing how good the Lord is when you pray and talk to Him. I recall visiting several churches where I knew no one there. I would listen to the sermons and try to get something from them, and then I'd make my usual stop after service and walk around the visitor's area and collect some of the pamphlets about Christ and being a Christian. I remember seeing a prayer box and how badly I felt about releasing all of my burdens. I was too ashamed to talk to anyone about what I was going through, so I discreetly put my name in the prayer box.

It really didn't matter at that point if I'd spoken to anyone at church, because I didn't trust that people cared. I only felt my own sorrow and pain and that's all I could handle. There were so many people that walked passed me to meet with someone they knew or were either talking with at the time. I didn't quite understand evangelism and how impactful it was in the body of Christ. I was naïve and lonely; I had no confidence in where to turn for help with my issues.

Some time had passed as I continued to wonder and pray for the answers to my prayers. I finally started seeing how real God was when He blessed me with a career job and giving me the strength to seek counseling for my marriage. But it was too late to salvage, because there was so many things to work through and compromise; therefore, I quietly moved forward toward the divorce process. I realized that I had to grow up and start trusting in God to help me get through it, as He promised in His word, "I will never leave you, nor forsake you."

I believe that the Lord allowed some trouble to come upon me, so that I would seek Him. Whatever mistakes were made I could no longer blame anyone. I needed to forgive my ex-husband and myself. We were married at a young age, while trying to raise a family. It was not easy for us to overcome our differences. I found the courage to see that God was putting everything together, so that I would be free. When it was time to walk away, the prayers that I needed answered were answered. There was no other way that I would have made it.

When you feel that there is no one to pray with you, fall down on your knees and pray to God right where you are. He is available and ready to hear from you. Don't delay because His angels are picking up new prayer requests daily.

CHAPTER 2

The Seeds of Hope, Faith, and Trust – Depression and Fear

Springtime was in the air and I could feel the warmth of the sun shining down on me; it propelled me to see why I needed to praise God for answering my cry and hearing my prayers. I moved out of the role of a wife into being single. I needed to learn how to believe in myself and make healthy decisions. I didn't know how to put my life together—it was in shambles—or where to begin to start loving myself and figuring out what I wanted to become. I faintly remember desiring to be a spiritual person; somehow I felt that it was empowering and liberating.

The fear of living alone felt frightening to me; it was the first time in my life. I learned some things fast and there were times when I felt frustrated because I didn't have the extra hands to help me hang new curtains and pictures, or to do handy things. I had to figure things out on my own; the things that I needed, I learned to buy assembled and have delivered. It lessened some of my frustrations, since I couldn't always find the help. But I was able to managed and get through it. It's amazing how God will give you the strength to get things done.

In retrospect, things appeared fine on the outside of my life, but the emotional scars, the fears, and tears were insurmountable. I continued to pray and talk to God about how I was feeling and how scared I was. There was a combination of people that I associated with. Some were already on their spiritual path in their quest to walk with God. Of course, I believed that God sent them my way for encouragement; we'd have small conversations about God, while sharing our faith. Also, I had friends whom I liked to hang out with and have fun partying.

The people that invited me to their church were only interested in converting me to their religion; but I needed a healing deep within my soul and I didn't feel anything by sitting in church. I noticed that they left me after I decided not to join their church. I'm not saying that church isn't good because it is a place where a body of believers gather weekly to fellowship and encourage each other in their faith. I suppose I wasn't ready to follow anyone, because I have had my share of walking in someone else's shadow. The phone calls and emails went away, and the visits ceased, too, for that matter. I was left alone and uncertain about whom to trust with my intimate feelings or the baggage and hurt that I was carrying. Behind closed doors, I was holding on by a thin rope with little hope, faith, and trust in God.

I surrounded myself with positive reading, inspirational books, meditation tapes, and music. Although I still read my Bible, I didn't use it daily, nor did I turn the pages enough to find the truth or answers to help me. My soul was going through a spiritual battle, and I didn't know it, but the Lord was there watching over me.

A few months after living in my apartment, I felt an accomplishment because I had everything that I needed at the time. I got a visit from an old friend; we talked a while and she told me about a guy that she thought was a nice person that I could be friends with. I remember feeling excited about the idea of having someone new in my life. Although I knew that I wasn't quite emotionally ready for what came with it.

After meeting Koz, things started out slowly between us. We talked until we became comfortable with each other. We'd go to dinner and the movies. I remember having a conversation over the phone with him about a matter on relationships and he disagreed with something I said. When he reacted brash, I became apprehensive about getting into a serious relationship with him and wanted to be assured if I should let go of pursuing any possibilities altogether. I shared my concerns with another friend about Koz's temperament and decided to take their advice to give him another chance.

I can recall it was on a Saturday morning when I woke up and heard a soft whisper: "Why do you feel like you need a man when I am supplying all your needs?" I pondered how blessed I was to have my freedom, own place, and the essential things that I needed, then suddenly I brushed off the words that were whispered to me.

While spending more time around Koz, I got to see the other side of his spirit. We'd be talking in general and all of a sudden, if we disagreed, he'd go on a rampage cussing, saying mean and insulting things to paint a bad picture on how relationships never work; his whole temperament was distorted. When he came around me I felt a negative energy from him. I could see that he was hurting too from a previous break up.

One day, the Lord sent a word to me through a prophet. The prophet was a friend of a friend of mine and he saw me in a picture that I had taken. My friend called me to relay the message that the prophet needed to give me a word from God. I arranged to meet with him at his church. He said, "The man that I was seeing was not my husband and God was sanctioning a God fearing man for me."

I desired to be married and Koz wanted a wife. But after I received the prophecy, I started to slowly understand how much God was instructing me to leave Koz alone. By that time he was irked and bothered by waiting for me to get my divorce on paper, so he could "date me properly," he'd say. I could feel his frustration and anger towards me, and I realized that I had been warned through the prophecy that he was not my husband. That's when my eyes became fully opened and I ran.

Although, I was not attending church on a regular basis, I was still praying and calling on Jesus to guide and protect me. It doesn't matter where we are in the world; God is present everywhere in the universe. He is closer than the air that we breathe; He knows everything about our past, present, and what's in our future.

Having hindsight about the things that I was going through, I perceive that it was ordained by God, because He continued to show me the way. I was not born again and my thought process was all carnal. I was looking for unconditional love, but I was too blind to see that it was God's love that was sustaining me the whole time.

Whenever we fall into various trials, trauma, emotional pain, and suffering, it's not easy knowing how to weed out the bad people in our lives. We tend to pick up friends easily when we're vulnerable, down, and depressed or when our thought process is destructive, negative, and confused. This is when the enemy sends all types of people to get us introduced to things that aren't good for us, i.e., drugs, alcohol, men, women, criminal activity, sexual immorality, etc. If you are going through something painful, believe that Satan is working on a plan to either attack or distract you from getting close to God. The devil knows that we are blinded by sin and that's why he works really hard to entice us.

Sometimes people mean well, but no one knows you like the Lord. It seems like when you are going through hard times, people tend to abandon you. It makes you feel isolated, destitute, and ashamed. That might be what God wants so that He can receive the glory and you will learn to trust and praise Him for rescuing you. Let the people talk; it doesn't mean anything when you have been chosen by God; He has to do a work in you and in order to prepare you, the tests are going to come. It doesn't matter what your past was; God has a way of bringing something good out of bad situations. The things that we go through make no sense sometimes, and they don't have to when God is in charge. We may have to experience some craziness in order to weed the wrong type of people out of our lives. Remember, it's all working together to manifest God's glory.

While I was at work, I met a new temporary employee. She was polite and I felt her pleasantness after our conversation. She was a Christian and single, too. So we started hanging around each other outside of work. I invited her over to my apartment and we would talk about our lives and faith at times. She was kind towards me and that made me feel comfortable around her, but little did I know that she was into astrology, psychics, and tarot cards.

During one of her visits, we sat down and she played a card game with me and read my future. It was interesting to see how she could shuffle a deck of regular cards and read into the future; she was passionate about what she believed. I was hesitant about her telling my future with a regular deck of "playing cards," but I went along with it; however, after that one encounter I wasn't interested anymore.

During work she stopped by my desk to ask me if I wanted to go with her to have my palm read. I thought about it since she had a coupon with a special discount to read both of our palms. I asked how much it cost, and she said it was only fifteen dollars, so I agreed to do it.

Still I wasn't strong enough to resist the devil; I met with a psychic and she spoke about my future husband and said that I was born to work for myself through my God-given talents and creativity. Everything sounded really good. Then she suggested that I come to her for a cleansing. She said that I needed a spiritual counselor to assist me in getting the things that I was predestined to receive.

On my second visit to the psychic, I brought the things that she asked me for. I was curious about how this business was helping people reach their dreams. I quickly came to my senses that it was through witchcraft. The cleansing was about paying more money, entangling my soul with the dark world. I stood up and told her that I shouldn't be there and that I was going to trust Jesus to lead me and I was not raised to go that way. I repented to God and ended things right away.

The things that I wanted from God were not going to come to me by the hands of the psychic, tarot cards, witchcraft, black magic, white magic, sorcery, mediums, voodoo, hoodoo, horoscopes, or any forces that were not sent by God. The Lord had predestined, before I was born, the blessings that were bestowed upon my life and how I would have to love, seek, obey, worship, and serve Him to receive my inheritance. These blessings are not manmade nor can they be substituted. I received that revelation from the Bible when I read it in the book of Proverbs 10:22. My soul needed healing, deliverance, and restoration. I needed my cup filled and overflowing with God's goodness and mercy.

Everywhere that I had turned away from God, I ran into more trouble and tests. I couldn't see straight if a bow and arrow had hit me. No one could have told me that there was a strong hold of demonic attacks assigned to me. The devil was on a mission to destroy my mind and soul. Many people can criticize someone else's weaknesses and ignorance, but what they cannot see is the evil spirit that's got you in a strong hold. Besides, everyone has some form of weakness within them, too.

When there is a calling on your life and you have been chosen, you are open to these kinds of attacks. These demonic attacks are stronger than your addictions and vices that entice you to sin. You cannot see the worst evil that's happening in the world with your physical eyes. In order for anyone to recognize it, one must have the spirit of discernment. If you are spiritually blind, it's impossible for you to lead the blind; there's not much help or insight that a person who's also blind could give to you when you're going through spiritual warfare, especially when you cannot recognize it in your own life.

These attacks just don't go away when people give you constructive criticism about your life. The advice could be practical and helpful—let's just say you've tried it—but somehow you keep falling back into the same rut or trouble; that's when spiritual discernment and deliverance is needed. The thing that people cannot understand is how to help you get deliverance from the evil spirit that's causing you to behave destructively. It's a spiritual work that needs to take place: fervently praying, having faith, and reading the word of God with strong intercessors, communing with God for your deliverance to destroy the yoke of the enemy.

The enemy wouldn't turn me loose; I was constantly under attack. People can call it what they want to, but if you cannot stop the bad things on your own that you're doing or going through, it's time to learn how to fight back, because Satan is real, and as long as you continue to feed your flesh with the things that are ungodly, he will continue to hold you tight in his grip.

My mind and everything within me wanted to give up. I cried and prayed to God for His Holy Spirit to dwell within me. I prayed for God to open my eyes and to give me the gift of discernment. I was tired of running and being the victim to the hands of people that I naively allowed into my life and chose to follow.

The people that came into my life for one reason or another manipulated me. I had no idea that I was so broken until I turned to retaliation. I was tired of being nice and I wanted to be the one to decide how much I would be used. My downfall was weeding out the bad men in my life, because I desired to be married. I felt that I would never find a good man if I didn't make myself available to anyone. So, I plotted a plan to date a new man every three months and drop him before things got bad. I realized that I didn't have enough experience to ensure that the plan would work. In retrospect, it was a dangerous road to travel.

Absolutely, I was certainly an open target, because the devil knew that my desire was to be married and he had his plan in motion by using his tactics, schemes, and trickery. I was not set free by God to run around loosely with different men or people to do my own thing. My physical eyes were open, but I was spiritually blind and walking dead; and like myself there are so many other women that fall prey to these same attacks.

I wrestled day and night in my spirit; I would sit back and think about all of the rotten things that happened to me. I was right where Satan wanted me. The only thing I could do at that point was pray. I reached out to a few people and asked them to pray over the phone for me. I did feel better after getting some prayer. I became extremely exhausted with trying to figure things out on my own or why things were going wrong. My battle was bigger than me. I could no longer fight with my own strength something that I could not understand.

At that point, my life was different. I had no more laughter, joy, and peace, nor did I like the person that I was becoming. I couldn't appreciate the sunny days anymore; therefore, I cried endlessly at home when the fear and pain pierced me the most. I felt that it was the safest place for me to be true to myself. My heart was filled with rage. Somehow, I ended up in worse conditions than before. I lost my hope, and faith; I was starting to wonder if God left me. Since, I continued to make a mess in my life, and I wondered to myself seriously where God was in all of this chaos.

CHAPTER 3

Turning to Prayer When No One Can Fix It – Sorrow and Repentance

As long as the sun shines and there's breath in our bodies, there is hope. It's natural to feel helpless when we can't fix our own problems or others', because God intended for us to depend on Him and to come to Him for all things. It's a one-sided relationship to turn to God only when we need His help after our lives are in a mess. Everything that happens to us, whether good or bad, doesn't surprise Him. He planned things out so that we don't miss out on knowing how much He loves, cares, and desires a relationship with those that love Him.

Sometimes, we aren't ready to listen or believe the talks, wisdom, advice, prayers from others that are given to spare us the pain or tragedy that may be waiting down the road. If we do not allow our pride to get in the way, the seeds of hope and faith will spring forth. We must be ready and willing to make the next step towards repentance, no matter how difficult things are.

The Lord placed my aunt on my heart, so I called her to ask for prayer. The words that she spoke aloud to God touched my heart as the tears fell. My soul was in desperate need of hearing someone else interceding and crying on my behalf to God. It connected me to her in a spiritual way. We would talk for hours, and she even got me to laugh at times. It felt good to let my guard down and to listen to a wise woman talk about the things that she went through and how the Lord kept her in the midst of her storms.

Sometimes, we don't know why we have to go through so many bad things, but each obstacle and test is ordained to point us in the right direction. It's a blessing to be able to talk to someone who's been through some near-death experiences and is still here to witness to others.

During my longest and darkest hours while fighting to keep my sanity, the storm was raging within me. I started praying for peace and hope again. When I stopped all of the dating and made a conscious decision to be still and seek God, I begin to turn the pages of the Bible and read more. I didn't understand a whole chapter when I would read different books of the Bible, so I would read scriptures that I was used to reading and the ones that my grandfather would read when I first accepted Christ. I needed to start someplace and these were my steps.

There were times when I did see some light in the midst of all the darkness. The light started to give me hope and strength. I remember going to Barnes and Noble on my lunch hour at work in search of a new Bible. The one that I had was still in good condition; I just wanted one that also had questions and answers for complex issues. I purchased the "*Woman's Life Bible.*"

I started reading my new Bible at home; some of the topics are friendship, marriage, parenting and family, personal concerns, single life, spiritual life, and work. These were important issues to me and the Bible pointed me to the right scriptures to help me gain more clarity and knowledge about the word of God.

When I was lost in the madness, I didn't know where to find scriptures to decree anything over my life nor enough scriptures that spoke to me on what I was going through. At first, I would read the Bible word for word when I read a scripture; nothing would get down on the inside of me. Therefore, I couldn't see how it could make my life problems better or how was I supposed to receive the power and blessings that are written in the Bible.

As Christians, we need to take the initiative to help others find the scriptures that will help them to start a new life with Christ. As we stand on what the word of God says, it is imperative that we are able to expound why we believe and must turn to the Bible to get the godly answers for every matter that pertains to life and mankind.

We cannot always hide behind someone else's knowledge about God. We see many Christians carrying their Bibles to church; but outside of church we need the word on the inside of us, so we are able to draw someone to Jesus. When we say that we are a Christian, no one knows it, until we are tried and tested or put into a situation in which God can use us to help someone.

People are not always willing to visit the church, especially when they are hurting. I could say that I was a Christian, but I only had a little word inside of me. I didn't know how to live by the word of God, because I didn't study his word nor memorize any scriptures to arm myself against the wiles of the devil. My emotions and flesh were leading me into a maze of confusion and spiritual darkness.

I became consciously aware that people with a bad spirit do nice things for others to lure them and to entangle them; they are capable of being manipulative by pretending to be something they are not. It's quite obvious that a God-fearing person would not want to be acquainted with a liar, thief, murderer, or an abuser, but how would we know how far to go with someone who approaches us if they seem to be kind, helpful, social, and charming? I can testify that this was how I got entangled many times with the wrong people. I wasn't being vigilant and prayerful in how I allowed the enemy to take up camp in my life.

I remembered how strong my heart was beating while the tears filled my eyes; I was battling with which direction I should go and hearing God's voice concerning the dilemmas in my life. I asked God to help me; I wrote down some of my thoughts and experiences. I went on a seven-day prayer consecration. Each day I would pray with a friend at 6:00 a.m. and at 9:00 p.m. I was faithful with the scheduled times. I kept a daily journal. On the fifth night while I was sleeping I remember opening my eyes and an angel was staring at me. When I begin to pray, it disappeared.

The Lord spoke these words to me at different times after my prayer consecration: "Denise, you must have faith. Don't look at a person's actions; look at their spirit. This will teach you how to discern spirits. You're not looking through the physical eyes, but being led by the Holy Spirit. Do not let your guard down by trusting the actions of a person. So many times women fall prey to it because they are lonely and these attacks are sent by Satan."

I was in pursuit of what God commanded me. I started reading the Bible faithfully, I believe, on April 10, 2002, with the book of John in the New Testament. One morning before getting out of bed, I could see and hear the words from the scripture: "Seek ye first the kingdom of God and all of his righteousness shall be added unto me" (Matthew 6:33). It continued to happen for days. I started feeling as though the Lord was talking to me, because the scriptures were vivid in my mind, as though I was looking into a mirror.

I felt God's presence all around me; it felt as though he wanted my attention and this time it worked. I was having a new experience with God and learning new Bible scriptures. My heart was lifted and I was in complete amazement about how God moved when I surrendered and asked Him for the help. I cried this time, because I was starting to see some profound things.

My search continued; I didn't want to let go of what I was experiencing with God. I was careful with whom I shared my feelings and thoughts. I didn't have time to question or doubt God by wasting time with seeking the opinions of people and other distractions. What was happening to me was quite clear; it was coming from within me. I continued to turn to God in prayer and wait for Him to speak to me through my dreams. This was the beginning of something new.

I believed the God of Abraham in the Holy Bible was actually revealing these things to me. I read about Abraham in Genesis chapter 12; the third verse stuck with me: "I will bless those who bless you, And I will curse him who curses you; And in you all the families of the earth shall be blessed." Jesus was the promised Messiah and he came from Abraham's lineage from the tribe of Judah. I received the revelation that I was a part of the families of the earth to be blessed, through accepting Jesus Christ as my Lord and Savior; I have been adopted by Jesus according to my faith and the scriptures: "For you are all sons of God through faith in Christ Jesus. For as many of you as were baptized into Christ have put on Christ. There is neither Jew nor Greek, there is neither slave nor free, there is neither male nor female; for you are all one in Christ Jesus. And if you are Christ's, then you are Abraham's seed, and heirs according to the promise" (Galatians 3:26–29).

There were not enough words in my vocabulary to explain it. I believe that God is always trying to get our attention, but we get so busy doing things that take our thoughts and time away from pursuing God. We know that the hand of God was upon us to have survived a fatal car accident, favor to get hired on a new job, acceptance into nursing school, blessings after blessings. Also, even when our backs are up against the wall and our hearts are turned towards God for prayer, it plants a seed of expectation, and when those prayers are answered, we start to believe that it was God that did it.

There are times when the signs aren't always obvious, i.e., meeting a kind stranger, a book that someone suggested that helped us, a referral to finding an attorney or physician, listening to our intuition. We tend to miss the signs when we aren't sober or ignoring the signs by calling things a coincidence. There is no such a thing when God is orchestrating all of the details in our lives. He's there in the background hoping that we turn to Him because He's reaching out with open arms to draw us close to Him.

I felt as though I was going backwards at times, instead of forward. I was encountering test after test; these unforeseen tests propelled me to seek God for why I kept repeating some of them. It's quite obvious that if someone fails a test, it's likely he or she will have to repeat it until they have a passing grade and can move on to the next level, reward, position, and/or promotion.

My aunt was always kind and supportive in helping me whenever I would reach out to her for prayer. I suppose that she must have grown tired at times by helping so many other people that called on her for spiritual help, too; therefore, she urged me to call her pastor who was a prophet for additional prayer. I agreed to call him, because she spoke kind words about him. She also asked me to send him a tithe or love offering for his time and work for helping me.

After speaking to my aunt's pastor on a few occasions, I sent him a tithe and letter to thank him and noted some of my prayer requests that I was waiting on God for. Since I was new to church protocol, I was hoping that maybe he would stand in agreement with me on my prayers. But I felt a hesitation in him; I didn't feel that there was a genuine kindness nor compassion in his spirit to do what he was doing for me, because the tempo in his voice would sound low as if he didn't want anyone to know that he was on the phone during the times that I had spoken to him.

Shortly after sending the letter to the pastor, I had a dream about the letter. I was in a house and it appeared to be some type of party gathering;

the people seemed to be family members and strangers playing cards and sitting around having a conversation. There were several small tables put together. I walked through this house and realized I didn't want to be there or felt it wasn't a place that I should be. As I walked towards the door a big, tall man in stature was standing there with a piece of paper in his hand. He spoke to me: "Those things can be, but I'm not ready yet!" I remember replying, "I know that."

The dream was certainly another sign, warning, or vision that God was preparing me for. I didn't understand how to talk about it to anyone, or actually how to proceed with trying to decipher the dream. It never crossed my mind to share it with my aunt, and I didn't want to dismiss or ignore it. So I decided to write it in my journal because I knew that it was another message or dream from God.

Additionally, I had shared with the Pastor a little about my life and some of the things that were hurting me: the divorce, dating, and the manipulation of being used by people. He listened enough to sum up what he thought was appropriate, then he mentioned how his wife was a strong woman and insinuated how I was weak and she wouldn't allow men to handle her in that way. When I got off the phone, I felt worse, ashamed, and I was done with him and turning to men for prayer.

I came to my senses that I let my guard down because I never felt led by God to him; it was a suggestion that my aunt felt would be a spiritual help to me. I knew that I was still hurting emotionally and the scars were deep. The last thing that I wanted was for someone to cast judgment on me and berate me while I was wounded. I couldn't see how he was helping me, but I noticed that he was happy when I sent him a donation. It was obviously not the path that God wanted me to follow.

Sometimes, when we are wounded, we put our trust in people that we believe can help us. Everyone that we confide in is not always capable to give us the help that we need; we can gain more insight and help from someone that has been in our shoes. If they have passed their tests, it's quite possible that they may be able to impart something inside of us that will lift our hearts and spirits to gain the hope to believe that we can make it through, if we hold on and apply the effective tools and steps toward receiving our breakthrough.

Surprisingly, the desire to be married didn't go away; I prayed for God to send me a God fearing husband, one that he had for me. I knew that this part of my life was where I needed much prayer, because each time I would get entangled with a man that was not my husband, my entire life would get turned upside down; new problems seemed to surfaced. I couldn't rest well at night, I had no peace of mind, and I had become so involved with analyzing everything because of falling into an unequally yoked relationship.

The time that I was spending and thinking about pleasing myself, I took my eyes off of God and away from following the path that was laid out for me. The devil knows how to dress up the very thing that isn't right for us to lure us away from the truth. Since having hindsight I would have tried harder to learn how to arm myself with the word of God and rebuke my flesh by staying away from the temptations, because it takes my participation to become entangled with the devil.

I could see how I lost my way because I wasn't spiritually matured in having discernment nor was I able to recognize that these were assigned distractions, attacks, and tests that I needed to overcome to get to the next level of discovering my purpose and following my destiny, but I had failed to take heed. It is frightening when you have some clue that you're being tested for the things that are divinely placed in your path.

I realized that my prayers or knowledge of the word were not strong enough to keep my flesh under control nor bind the negative thoughts. I just didn't know how to get into that place with the Lord long enough to remain steadfast, so that the enemy and his vices wouldn't lead me astray. My soul was barren and weary.

During a spiritual battle, we have no idea what is happening, because we're trying to analyze things with logic and reasoning and brushing things off; but we can't, because it's a spiritual attack. We may think that we're fighting with ourselves through our emotions being out of control and our thoughts going awry, but we're also fighting the principalities and powers that Satan used to entice us away from our walk with the Lord. The flesh is going through a war because it's used to doing things the old way by listening to our ego and being enslaved to sin. The Satanic spirit that was holding me bound didn't want to turn me loose.

When the Lord is trying to do a work in us the process is spiritual and it can take a long time; many years and seasons may pass before we can see any fruit in our lives. There are so many intricate details that must take place before a purging goes forth, i.e., ending ungodly relationships and habits; changing our circle of people, places, and things; renewing the mind with the word of God; separation before elevation, consecration, and sanctification; and being filled with the Holy Spirit. When it comes to spiritual work, it's not wise to say how God will do this or that, nor how He will handle the next person, because His thoughts are not like man nor are His ways like man. The Lord may choose to work in someone else's life in a different way in order to prepare them.

My will in surrendering to God was strong when my heart and soul were in pain; but when I started to feel better again, my old mind would creep back in by reminding me of the things that I used to do, and what my flesh wanted. My mind would drift back and forth about marriage and how being equally yoked with the right man was the answer to knowing that I had found the right man. But I wasn't able to see the whole picture of how God was pulling me out of darkness every time I got entangled with someone. I didn't trust Him enough to wait and follow His divine plan because I just kept getting in the way.

Our happiness and peace of mind does not depend on outward things or someone else outside of God. I was still trying to figure things out with my finite mind, while God was drawing me close to him by forming an intimate relationship with me.

CHAPTER 4

Spoken Prayers – Seeking God

*T*he earth rejoices when it rains because there are so many blessings that fall upon the earth. The planet is rejuvenated by the moisture in the air; green life is restored and enriched; crops are yielding; the flowers and plants are able to bloom and cultivate; while every living creature is replenished by nature's oxygen and water.

Every seed that has been planted yearns to be watered while it remains covered and protected. As the seed grows on good ground, its roots are forming within the earth. The rain that it receives brings forth the fruit of what type of seed is sown. As with a mustard seed, it's tiny in size, but once it reaches the capacity of freedom, its stature cannot be thwarted.

It had been five years since my last mammogram. I remembered the experience as if it were yesterday; while I was taking a shower, I noticed some bleeding. Suddenly, I turned the water off to examine where the bleeding was coming from; it was my breast. I took a deep breath and exhaled deeply while my heart started throbbing. I started to panic as the thought of cancer crept into my mind.

My maternal grandmother died of breast cancer. When I was in my early twenties I was diagnosed with fibrocystic breast disease. I had always feared it and didn't understand it. However, the incident had awakened a fear that was buried down inside of me for years; the thought of cancer and every thought from there became overwhelming to me. I shared the experience and my fears with a friend and she urged me to see the doctor. There was hesitation on my part and she could hear the fear in my voice, so she offered her support to go with me to the hospital.

As I reflect on a time, I had another friend who I had known for a long time and was battling breast cancer. Although I knew her story when she first detected a lump, I started feeling as though I could be next. As she was battling with her illness and coming to terms with having cancer, she became critical of me; I couldn't understand it or why her behavior changed.

We never talked about what really happened between us, but she felt that I wasn't spending enough time with her. I didn't understand how to do that with a volatile marriage at the time, but we did remain cordial when we did speak over the phone and when we saw one another.

I never wanted to see her go through the pain nor did I want to abandon our friendship, but the handwriting was on the wall. She had gotten married and didn't invite me to the wedding. I wasn't surprised but I was hurt. She would talk about her new friend that she had replaced me with, the new career, and home. She shared some of her struggles that she went through during her eighteen-hour surgery. I would listen to her talk, because I knew that I couldn't be there for her in the way that she wanted me to be. There was no need for me to say anything because I was already fighting with a different battle that took me down a different path.

I now understand that if I had had a closer walk with Jesus, I could have imparted my prayers and encouraging words into her spirit, or maybe exhibited my value as a friend. It could have changed the course of action in how things turned out between us before she lost the battle to breast cancer.

On my second visit to the hospital after discovering bleeding from my breast, I was returning this time to find out my test results from the mammogram. While I was sitting and waiting for my name to be called, all of a sudden I needed to use the washroom, and as I walked toward the washroom, my sight became distorted, very blurry, so I leaned against the wall close to me to help guide my footsteps. I couldn't see the faces of the people that were talking and walking opposite of me, nor could I make out the words that were called out over the intercom.

When I made it to the door of the washroom, my ears had become plugged, and everything seemed dark and faint. I started reciting aloud the 23 Psalms: "*The Lord is my Shepherd, I shall not want.*" I didn't have enough strength to push the door open or pull on it, but I could faintly see that there was someone walking towards me. I had my hands and arms out in front of me while trying my best to feel my way into a stall. As soon as I sat down, I was pulled off of the toilet seat by a woman. She put some cold wet paper towels on my face, and with the help of a man, I was wheel-chaired to a room in the back so that I could be seen by the doctor.

There were no new changes in my x-ray images; therefore, I was released from the hospital. The doctors couldn't explain why I had the bleeding from my breast, or the other bizarre incident that I had in the washroom at the hospital. At first, I thought that it may have been the stress and anxiety that I was harboring, and it was starting to manifest in my body. I started to understand that things don't just happen for any apparent reason; later I learned that my friend who had cancer passed away on the same day I was at the hospital. I felt as though something left my spirit that day.

I made amends in my heart before she passed away, but I failed at doing it in person by expressing my feelings through a card. However, she never received it because her family had moved. Through my friend's passing I realized that I couldn't undo how I did things after our friendship changed when she fell sick. I wanted to be there more than I tried but my life was in a mess. She was the friend who I reached out to when I attempted suicide, and by her urgency, I listened to her and got to the hospital in time to be saved. I couldn't see how I would have been very strong for her nor handle seeing her suffer and not being able to reach or bring comfort to her life. I believe that she was sent into my life to help me find my way when I no longer knew which way to go.

I went through my time of grief and needed to forgive myself for disappointing her by not always coming to visit and by not showing great concern in the details of her day-to-day struggles with her disease. Through time I was able to move past feeling guilty and confused about what happened in our friendship.

Some people are a season in our lives and are sent to us because they are assigned to fulfill a need. When their purpose, assignment, and season is over, they must continue on their journey. Therefore, I accepted God's will and love and the fact that He was healing me from the hurt feelings that I was harboring over the loss of my friend.

Since reflecting upon the experiences that I had gone through with my friend dying of breast cancer, I knew that it was time to face my biggest fear again: going back to the doctor for my annual mammogram. I wanted to move forward, but the fear of not having my annual mammogram tests five years after I encountered bleeding from my breast seemed insurmountable. Somehow, I found the courage, along with my prayers, to become proactive in knowing how my health was doing.

I went to the hospital to get my mammogram on May 4, 2002. I received a call from the hospital to come back to get retested. I wanted to trust God and believe that I was going to be all right, but there was a part of me that kept saying I had the chance to know what my health condition was concerning my breast; however, I ran from the truth.

Whenever I would think of any negative thoughts about my health, I would combat it by thinking of how good God was to me. I would turn to my aunt for prayer, and every time that she would pray for me aloud, I would cry out to God to have pity on my soul.

During the two weeks, I prayed continuously to God about having a good praise report from the doctors. The night before I went back to the doctor's office to get my test results, I asked God to show me a sign in my sleep that he was looking down upon me. I remember waking up in my bed looking toward the ceiling, where I could see a cloud of water and hear the words, *"Denise, the kind of thoughts you think and believe is the type of energy you will bring into your life!"* I knew that this was the confirmation that I needed to continue walking by faith.

I returned to the hospital on May 14, 2002. The doctor reviewed the x-rays on the screen and gave me the news that the growth they had seen a few weeks ago had moved. She could no longer see it on the x-ray image! My heart was beating calmly because I was finally able to let go of the fear that I had been carrying for such a long time.

I thanked the doctor after receiving my final paperwork; then, I walked out of the doctor's office and I humbly thanked God for his miraculous move and mercy in my life. When I got into my car I bowed my head and went into a deep thought of gratitude—God does answer prayer.

My heart was full of awe because I couldn't stop thinking about the signs and wonders that God was revealing to me. As I realized that all things are possible with God, the feeling of being loved and thought about by God was blowing my mind. He was teaching me to follow him, to seek his righteousness, and to give all of my worries and troubles to him. The light was shining down on me, illuminating the way that I should go; the tears were coming from my soul because I was grateful.

When the doctor tells us that they need to do additional tests, it doesn't matter what their report says; even if they rule it out and there is a condition, the Bible tells us in Matthew 19:26, "But Jesus looked at them and said to them, 'With men this is impossible, but with God all things are possible.'" The Lord wants us to follow him with all our heart. He doesn't want us to run away from him, but towards him.

The enemy works on our minds day and night by trying to persuade us to think that we have everything under our control. His job is to isolate us from each other and to keep our minds busy with nuisance and filled with distorted view points, negative thoughts, fear, and lies. He takes camp inside of hurting people by using our past to keep us captive to his devices. The mind is the battlefield where Satan takes control over a person's life. We must be on guard at all times to know how to fight back with the word of God by reading, studying, and praying the word over our thoughts, minds, bodies, and lives. It's a constant mission to become conscious and spiritually mature in knowing when he is at work in our lives.

I was guilty because I allowed my fear of going to the doctor to get in the way of seeking God for the answers and allowing Him to be the strength that I needed. He is in complete control over what happens to us, although I didn't understand this revelation until some years later because I was not able to see nor understand that my problems were designed for me to run to Jesus; He was illuminating His light, and yet I still had more hills to climb and valleys to travel.

The journey is a discovery process of learning lessons, finding our life purpose, identifying who we are in Christ, praying to know him, and learning how to love, serve, and worship God the way that He desires us to.

Sometimes, we want to get upset with God when a certain thing doesn't work in our favor, or we end up with a different outcome than we expected; but no matter what, we must chose to follow Christ and be willing to work our faith in all seasons. The just shall live by faith and we must be willing to share our testimony, good or bad, even when it seems like there is no possible solution to the matter. That is why the word of God is written—so that we the believers must agree with the word, get the word inside of our mouths, minds, behavior, and hearts.

When Jesus came to the earth, He knew that God sent Him; His mission was to fulfill His purpose and to give up His life as the sacrifice for the atonement of our sins so that all mankind could be reconciled back to God. Jesus experienced long suffering, pain, fear, hurt, tears, hate, ridicule, humiliation, and so much more. The worst was He died a crucifixion death; He was hung, His blood was shed, and He died minute by minute for us. He was perfect and there was no sin found in him. He was the promised Messiah, and He came to earth to save us from condemnation and eternal death, and to offer us salvation and eternal life when we accept Him as Lord and Savior over our lives.

We are going to experience difficult times and some of the same pain and hurt; there's just no way around it. We have been warned through the Bible about the world in which we live. Therefore, we must study the Bible to know the truth and to discern spiritual things that we are not capable of knowing or able to see through our natural eyes without being instructed by the word of God and the Holy Spirit.

There are many denominations in the faith to become a part of, but remember that there is only one Lord, one Faith, and one Baptism. We must follow Jesus and study His life in order to know how we should live. The Bible tells us in the book of Romans 10:9:10 how to be saved. I've learned what the Bible tells me about being saved. It is written in the word what one must do to be saved. If we are adding to the word, then anything in addition to it is considered a sin, one's opinion, experience, and doctrine.

Some people have added their version to this topic on getting saved based upon their church doctrine or theory. Some say that we must speak in tongues, and others say without the evidence of tongues a person is not saved. In other words, this seems to be a deal breaker for some; but if a person doesn't speak in tongues, it should not prevent them from being loved and accepted into the faith. We are not God, and those who do speak in tongues should not think that they're any closer to Jesus, because tongues do not save a person from eternal hell; rejecting Jesus is the deciding truth to refusing salvation.

The power belongs to God, and when He is ready and sees fit for anyone to speak in tongues, then He will impart that supernatural power and gift upon them. I'm not speaking against the day of Pentecost in the book of Acts 2:1–13 when they were all together in one place and a sound like a violent wind from heaven blew upon them and the people were filled with the fire of baptism. This scripture was a promise that Jesus spoke to His disciples and believers that waited to be filled with His power and Spirit to continue in the works that He promised they would do in His name. They spoke in tongues and in many languages to spread the gospel of Jesus Christ and were given the power to heal the sick among them that spoke different languages and never knew Christ, so that they would be compelled to believe and accept their gift of salvation in Christ. Also, speaking in tongues is a spiritual gift that one may receive to use as their heavenly language when they are praying to the Father.

In the meantime, if you have accepted Christ as your Lord and Savior and are baptized, continue seeking to know who Jesus is through a prayerful life and bible study. I am saved, and no one can prevent whom God has chosen to save. The word never changes, and the scripture tells us, in Hebrews 13:8, "Jesus Christ is the same yesterday, today, and forever." In 1 Corinthians 1:10, we are told, "Now I plead with you, brethren, by the name of our Lord Jesus Christ, that you all speak the same thing, and that there be no divisions among you, but that you be perfectly joined together in the same mind and in the same judgment."

When we walk with Jesus, there's nothing that will separate us from His love, and His power is enough to keep us. Once we accept Jesus, then we can put our total trust in Him to do the work through the Holy Spirit to reveal to us who Christ is and our identity in Christ and plant us where we are to bloom. It's all a process and a lifestyle as we grow from being infants to mature Christians in the word. Praying to know who Jesus is and learning about His life will yield fruit and prosperity in having a sound mind to fulfill one's life purpose.

My aunt would call me from time to time to give me some encouragement. She would urge me to join a Bible-believing-and-teaching church. I became active in my search to find a church that I could attend and grow in my walk with the Lord. I perused through the yellow pages first, and then I saw the name of a church that I remembered in a community where I once traveled. I felt compelled to start there, attending the Bible classes and service on Sundays.

One Sunday during service, the church announced that there was a luncheon for the new members after service. I felt comfortable there, so I decided to attend. The majority of the tables were filled, so I sat alone. When I lifted my head, there was a tall man in stature asking if he could sit with me. There were a few more tables empty, but he asked to sit at mine. I didn't want to stare back at him, but I took a small glance when he wasn't looking.

While everyone was engaging in conversation with each other and eating their food, the gentleman introduced himself as Shamir to me. He started by saying that he'd been looking for a wife since 1996. I politely responded that he needed to be patient and wait on God. My spirit started to change because my flesh started rising. So, I decided to turn away from him while I rebuked my flesh. When the luncheon was over, on my way out the door, I heard the pastor asking him if he had found a job.

A few weeks later, I was in a car accident only seconds away from being a head-on collision. When my car was struck in the middle of the intersection, the experience was surreal; I remember my car stopping and smoke was coming from the air bag under the steering wheel. I crawled out of my car to the ground and started praising God for covering me. The other driver's car had hit a pole and she had passed out. Once again the Lord had spared my life; I was able to walk away from the accident without fatal injuries.

I remembered anointing myself with oil and saying a prayer aloud to God the morning of the accident. Also, I remembered how I walked down to the altar at church to receive prayer the Sunday before the accident. I was able to see more clearly how God was protecting me and that my steps were ordered by the Lord.

After being released from the hospital, I went on part-time medical leave from work for two months, and I had to attend several sessions of physical therapy. I shared my testimony with anyone that inquired or had heard the news about my accident; however, by their response, I could tell that they didn't understand my faith, and I wasn't willing to accept their comments about my outcome from the accident, e.g., my car was too old and I wouldn't get much for it; I couldn't afford to pay my rent with part-time hours; I wouldn't be able to get around without a car; it was going to be hard to prove who was at fault in the accident; plus, a law suit was going to be impossible to win. Secretly, I had previously changed my insurance coverage from comprehensive to only liability on my vehicle a few weeks before the accident.

The Lord wiped away my tears during the night of the accident and gave me the courage to believe that everything was going to be alright. I received a call that evening from the woman that struck my car in the accident; I remember giving her my phone number when she stopped by my room at the hospital. She wanted to know how I was doing and cooperated by giving me everything that I needed to get compensated for the accident. But of course, it was her fault because she drove right passed the stop sign; therefore, her car hit mine head on. The insurance company told her to not speak to me at all about the accident. I cried when I heard this because God was showing me that His love was for me and that He did not leave me.

The outcome was in my favor and I was blessed to receive a substantial check in the mail for my old car and purchase another car in little time. During my medical leave I was able to rest and have ample funds to pay my bills. I was in awe that my entire income had tripled during the time; I didn't need to borrow any money from family or friends. However, I was so amazed when I checked my mailbox and I had received a check from a relative.

Although things were working out for my good, there was something missing—I felt lonely being at home during my recovery. I hardly received any phone calls; it was quiet and different for me at home. I wanted to feel the assurance that I was loved and talk about my experience from the accident. My children were supportive in the best way they knew. I was blessed to have family support that did come through for me when they heard the news, and for that, I am still grateful.

Sometimes when we are left alone, we tend to see it as a setback, loss, or inconvenience. These times are critical because God knows how to redirect our steps and renew our minds, although it's quite scary when things are shaken apart in our lives. We must believe that God has His arms covering us in everything that happens to us; He is guiding us towards the plan that He has prepared for our lives.

While I was at home still recuperating from the accident, I received a delivery of flowers. The church sent them to inform me that they were praying for my healing. The flowers were beautiful and fresh. It really did brighten up my day. It felt good to be connected to the church because their work was touching lives. I didn't know how they knew about my accident, but I was humbled and thankful that they reached out to me in my time of need.

I later learned that Shamir had told the church about my accident during one of the services. When I went on medical leave, I set up all my email accounts to notify everyone that I would be out of the office. Shamir was on the distribution list, and that's how he was able to know about the accident.

Shortly after, I received a phone call at home from Shamir; he had found my number listed in the white pages. I wasn't happy about it, but I remained cordial and polite. He was concerned about me and wanted to see if I needed anything. His phone call made me remember how I was feeling lonely and how I wanted someone to talk to, but I quickly realized that I didn't know him.

When I returned to church, I remembered seeing Shamir after service. He was helping the other staff members move chairs outside for the church's picnic that day. When he passed by me to say hi, I noticed a huge difference in his weight across his shoulders; he looked slimmer. It was quite noisy that day because of the church's picnic, but I felt a slight pulling in my stomach; faintly I could hear the words, *"he is still using drugs; don't believe him."* At the time, I didn't believe it was the Holy Spirit speaking to me because I was not trained to listen nor trust in Him; therefore, I ignored it.

The Lord is always intervening in our lives; sometimes there's a soft whisper or tug in our spirits. But when we don't yield or listen, nor take out the time to get into a quiet place and seek God about these distractions and warnings, we are going to have to walk through the fire. Some of us are comfortable about running to the phone to share every little detail that we encounter. Sometimes that cannot save us because we still end up going through situations that God has already ordained regardless of whom we may know that can help us.

Some of us have walked right into the lion's den and sat down with the enemy, knowing that we were supposed to run and go the other way. It is God's will to save, protect, and teach us about the enemy's plan. The Bible warns us in John 10:10, "Thief does not come except to steal, and to kill, and to destroy. I have come that they may have life and that they may have it more abundantly."

I was a little sheep wandering around, trying to find a place to dwell and grow in the word of God. It was important for me to pursue what God was revealing to me, but when it came to my flesh and the weakness that is within me, it became another battle because the war was within me. I wanted to follow Jesus because He is the good shepherd and I needed Him to cover me from the hurt and harm. I didn't understand the parables that He taught in the Bible, but I knew that He was someone that I could learn to love and trust because He is the Son of God; I thought if only I could stop falling into these snares I could live the life that Jesus died for me to have serving Him.

Since that day of the church's picnic, I started having more dialogue with Shamir; it turned into walks in the park, dinners, outings, and romance. Several months had passed by when he asked me to marry him; he wanted me to promise that I would. I didn't know how to respond because my mind reverted back to the words that I had heard in my dream: *"That those things can be, but I'm not ready yet!"*

My aunt came to visit me for a few days during my recovery from the accident. She went with me to church, and that's when I introduced her to Shamir. I vaguely remembered how much I had told her about Shamir before her visit, except that he told me God said that I was his wife. She wasn't saying much to me, but I believed it was because she was allowing the Holy Spirit to discern to her what to say about me and Shamir.

After service we decided to go out to dinner at a Chinese restaurant. As we were walking back to our cars, she asked Shamir if it was okay to pray for him and he agreed. She spoke into his life and gave him some encouraging words of what God was revealing to her. She told him that if he stayed in church and continued to walk with the Lord that God would raise him up in five years to be a great man. He gazed at her intently as though he received it.

Some weeks later, Shamir's proposal was weighing heavily on my mind. Suddenly the phone rang, and it was my aunt calling to pray for me; she spoke these words: *"Denise don't make any promises to your friend."* I was in complete shock because of the timing, and the words that she spoke to me brought back to my memory the dream that I had.

She said that, despite whatever was going on between me and my friend, the Lord wanted her to tell me those words. Ironically, Shamir was sitting close by me when I answered the phone. I didn't know how to wiggle my way out of it, but I knew what she meant by those words and that I had better say something soon.

I had gotten entangled with helping him modify his resume and allowed him to stay at my apartment when he had nowhere to go because his living arrangements had changed. He was no longer staying with the family at the church because he was spending the majority of his time with me.

His work was part time and seasonal. He had to find a different plan because the original one wasn't working anymore. It was going to take a while before he could afford to pay for the wedding ring he had put on layaway. Things were at a standstill; I was unsure of what I needed to do; I was emotionally attached to helping him more than being in love. He would throw comments at me, saying that if I loved him I would help him and be patient until things got better, but I started feeling the toll that it had taken on me.

My entire life had changed; I gave away my joy and peace that God had blessed me with. I couldn't enjoy the simple things in life anymore: my nice apartment, freedom, travelling, walks in the park with God, having my privacy at home, and splurging on myself. My soul was eroding inside because the bad choices I had made revealed that I was sacrificing my happiness for the sake of being married. I didn't like the snapshot of how being married to him looked; therefore, it gave me the strength to slowly pull away from him and start working on an exit plan.

My greatest fear was dealing with his anger and listening to him while he distorted the truth about why his life was in a deficit and had turned out the way it did. In the past, I observed a few times how he would get upset and lash out with mean and hurtful words towards other people that had hurt or failed him. I didn't want to become one of those people, but I knew that I couldn't promise him that I would marry him or be waiting for him when he got his life together. It was far too much to continue sacrificing and putting my soul through; I realized that I had dug myself into a pit from hell.

Shamir didn't want to walk away from me when he was down on his luck; he waited until he was gainfully employed and at the top of his game. When I saw the arrogance and meanness coming out, I was willing to end all contact with him; however, it was too late by then because he was so bent on harming me and blaming me for the relationship not working.

When I gave him the rest of his things, he didn't look well. He didn't want to leave peacefully. He sat down and started talking about how he tricked me; he had other women that would have married him, but he wasted too much time on me. Then, he threatened to throw me off of my apartment balcony. My stomach dropped at this time; I felt the fear and fright hitting me all at once in the chest. I was able to see that everything I had been warned about him was out in the open. I was scared out of my wits, and underneath my breath, my throat and heart were throbbing fast. As I stared back at him, I held back my tears and the fear. Then, my mind went into another zone; I remembered praying to the Holy Spirit to help me and pleading for God's mercy to come see about me. The Lord didn't allow him to see the fear that I had. He covered me with His Spirit and put His words into my mouth. I remember Shamir getting up out of his chair and walking towards the door.

During the course of time, Shamir realized that I wasn't going to marry him, and towards the last few months of seeing him, he found employment and wanted to brag about it to me. He would call me sporadically to tell me about his new apartment, car, and job. I did some snooping and found out that he did get hired, but he didn't make it through the probation period due to missing work. I called his phone one Friday evening and another man answered it. I knew immediately that he was back into the drugs and street life because he was so paranoid about staying away from those negative people who were into illegal activities and the drinking and partying scene. He told me at the beginning that he was going to be honest with me and tell me the things that he was doing in the streets that caused him to spiral out of control, as well as the triggers luring him back into that life.

Somehow, he got into my apartment building while I was at work and managed to put nasty notes on my apartment door and the laundry room, threatening to tell my secrets to the people that hurt me. He wouldn't stop at trying to harm or humiliate me; therefore, I had to get my ex-husband,

Shamir's family, and neighbors involved. I contacted my human resources to stop him from coming to my work, where he'd leave nasty letters on my car and envelopes with the receptionist.

The devil does not like it when you expose him. He'll do all kinds of things to fight you back so that you will not get away. But I was willing to fight back and get the protection that I needed. It turned into a vicious cycle of intimidation, manipulation, and wickedness that I couldn't get out of quickly.

I've learned that real unconditional love is when the people you have in your life are willing to help you in some way or another when times are bad or good. The greatest power sometime is prayer either over the phone or in person because we are battling with spirits. The Holy Spirit teaches us how to pray and what to pray; when we obey and pray aloud, it sets the atmosphere to bind the enemy and his demons, and it releases the power to destroy the yoke and cancels out all of Satan's attacks that are trying to take over our mind and soul.

The devil cannot do anything with a prayer warrior; they are equipped to die on the battlefield for our victory. The Lord is dispatching angels when he hears our spoken prayers. In Psalms 103:20, the word teaches us, "Bless the Lord, you His angels, Who excel in strength, who do His word, Heeding the voice of His word." We have scriptures to arm ourselves against the powers, darkness, and rulers in high places of this world and other dominions to decree a thing. In Isaiah 54:17, we find, "No weapon formed against us shall prosper." The enemy may form it, but it will not prosper. The one who gets the final word over a thing is God, and He says in Isaiah 55:11, "So shall My word be that goes forth from My mouth; It shall not return to Me void, But it shall accomplish what I please, And it shall prosper in the thing for which I sent it."

Of course, I was that blind sheep that the Bible talks about; I was that wounded sheep that kept going astray. In the book of Luke 15:3, the Bible tells us, "So He spoke this parable to them, saying: 'What man of you, having a hundred sheep, if he loses one of them, does not leave the ninety-nine in the wilderness, and go after the one which is lost until he finds it? And when he has found it, he lays it on his shoulders, rejoicing. And when he comes home, he calls together his friends and neighbors, saying to them, "Rejoice with me, for I have found my sheep which was lost!" I say to you that likewise there will be more joy in heaven over one sinner who repents than over ninety-nine just persons who need no repentance.'"

Through my thorns and tests, the Lord was helping me to see that He was building an intimate relationship with me. Since my heart was fixated on getting married, He had to get my attention to let me know that there is no happiness outside of the will of God. He was blowing His breath of life into my nostrils every day and putting clothes on my back, feeding me, healing me from all of my sicknesses and diseases, and rescuing me from the snares in which I would get entangled, wiping away my tears, and giving me favor and the victory in every battle that I have to face.

In spite of my disobedience to God, I know now why God revealed the dream to me: so that I would learn to obey Him and heed His warnings and to trust the Holy Spirit. The Holy Spirit does not lie to us; we must understand that He is a teacher, companion, counselor, comforter, and exhorter, convicting us when we are wrong, protecting us from Satan's lies, revealing the truth in all things, and drawing us back into the ark of safety when we stray or fall out of the will of God.

Sometimes, we may have to go through bad situations in order for God to show His mighty power that He is in our lives. There is no other way to teach us a spiritual lesson than to go through a spiritual test. Since I didn't listen, I felt as though I did not pass mine and that there was no redemption for me; but as the scales fell from my eyes, I was able to witness the power of spoken prayers operating in my life. In spite of my disobedience, God saw fit to rescue me.

CHAPTER 5

A Prayer List Sent to Heaven
– Submission to God's Will

Everyone has bad days, but it's harder to bear them when the guilt weighs heavily on our conscience. Sometimes when we replay things over and over again in our minds, we're trying to convince ourselves that we didn't know any better, that it wasn't our fault things happened the way they did, or we wished that we could do things differently. Instead of dwelling on the past and thinking about our excuses, we must believe that there is a reason why we go through life's ups and downs. Primarily, when we move past our failures, hurts, disappointments, and obstacles, we are becoming better people.

Since the previous test that I was given, I realized that I should have taken heed to the signs and warnings that God was showing to me. My heart was shattered into broken pieces while I carried the guilt and anguish around within me. Again, I didn't know how to get my life back on track, but this time I could subtly see that my mind was turning away from being married to seeking the purpose to my life.

While I was seeking the answers to why I was having so many bad experiences in my life, the emotional pain was piercing to my soul. It caused me to feel overwhelmed by my feelings of guilt and the lies and the manipulation that went on about the recent nightmare. When the tears fell, I would say that *"this too shall pass,"* because God didn't make two days the same. I may cry today, but tomorrow could be the beginning of a new chapter in my life.

When we feel broken and helpless, that's when God can do His best work in us. He was preparing me for something that was beyond what I had prayed for. I remember trying to conceal the nightmare, but my smile was fading. It was senseless to talk about it in detail, because I didn't want to hear how stupid I acted, although it was tearing me apart. Therefore, I turned my focus towards a new project at work that required long work days and some weekends.

The overtime was the right distraction because the project that I was working on required my attention to detail. I practically worked every weekend. Things did slowdown in my social life, until one day I had lunch with a co-worker. She introduced me to the book *"Purpose Driven Life"* by Rick Warren. I felt compelled to read it after seeing the book's title and making a connection with how passionately the author declared that everyone had been given a purpose in life. I was enthralled, and immediately, I rushed out to the store to buy my own copy.

It was around fall of 2003, when I was invited to attend a T.D. Jakes conference. I went to the conference seeking something, and I heard him speak his testimony of how God gave him a dream and he followed God's instructions until it manifested into a phenomenon *"Woman, Thou Art Loosed"*. I felt energized while listening to him; I believed that it was ordained for me to be at the conference that evening, because something was ignited within me.

Since I was making more money with the overtime, I would treat myself by going out to dinner, attending concerts, and shopping for a new wardrobe. It felt safe and it became easier for me to cope with the loneliness. I avoided crowds and any social circle because I realized that I needed the time to focus on my healing and face the things I was suppressing that caused me pain. I became somewhat a recluse through the process.

I continued to contemplate my own life and reflect on the things that I wanted to do before I leave earth. I would go back and forth with setting some goals; I remembered that I had written some poems and had started writing a book about my life before I got entangled with the last relationship. My writing was put on hold for a year and a half. I meditated on the words that

I had written in my poems. It evoked some feelings inside me that caused me to reminisce about when I was a little girl writing short stories in my diary. I had thought about becoming a songwriter when I was in high school. I knew that I had a vivid imagination of doing something creatively in life, and it helped me to escape my tumultuous childhood.

Several months had passed; I still felt lonely and my soul continued to cry out to God for comfort. The pain was sharp like small needles traveling to my heart. I wanted it to end. I found comfort in listening to my favorite gospel songs, which helped me to hold on to my belief that God was real. I realized that I didn't know Him personally, but I believed that my faith and His word were carrying me from day to day.

I stayed in touch with a cousin who had gotten a divorce around the time I went through mine. She called to tell me about a woman that she had met who was a prophet. The prophetess had given her some words of encouragement and it blessed her life. I asked if she could put me in touch with the prophetess for prayer.

She connected the three of us via conference call. When the prophetess spoke into the phone, she began to speak about some intimate things that only God knew about me. She spoke about the devastating things that I was struggling with and phrasing certain words which brought back to my memory the scripture Jeremiah 29:11.

Something on the inside of me leaped because my heart started beating faster. As she continued to speak, the words were flowing from her mouth. She had my undivided attention; I could feel myself reaching up to hold on to every word. I was amazed at how God was moving through her. I had never met her nor did my cousin know anything about my situation or any of the details that I was concealing.

When I hung up the phone, I was in a stupor; no one could have known that much about me without knowing God. It was indeed a divine revelation that was given to me, reserved for such a time as this.

I remember the next day, a Saturday, was the first time I heard God's voice; while I was sleeping, God spoke to my spirit, *"I will create in you a new spirit!"* I heard it clearly; the voice resonated and vibrated through my being. When

I opened my eyes it was morning; I remember staring at the ceiling above my canopy bed. My mind was in a trance as I pondered those words that I heard.

The Bible tells us in 2 Corinthians 5:17, "Therefore, if anyone is in Christ, he is a new creation; old things have passed away; behold, all things have become new." The words that God had spoken to me were from the scripture. I was astonished by the move of God because I had never thought that He could speak to me nor reveal His Spirit to me; I never fathomed it. My prayers were sent to Heaven but this one topped them all; it revived new life into me which caused things that were happening in the natural part of my life to align with the supernatural order of things that were ordained by God.

On that Sunday, the same weekend that I heard God speak to me, my cousin and I called Prophetess Hopewell to tell her the news. She prayed for me again and began to tell me more things that the Lord was going to do in my life. She spoke about God having an anointing on my life. At the time, I broke down crying because it was surreal.

My mind drifted away for a moment; while pondering the times when I called my aunt for prayer and while she was praying in tongues, I didn't understand her heavenly language until she would say what the Holy Spirit was saying to her about how God was preparing me for a work to do. During this time, I withheld revealing any intimate things about myself to Prophetess Hopewell because I wanted my experience with her to remain authentic and pure and to allow God to speak through her when He wanted her to minister to me.

During the next conversation I had with Prophetess Hopewell, she immediately started speaking, *"The Lord is shaping me and I am a bud at this time; when my season comes to do the work of the LORD, I will be a flower. He will prepare me for His work."* She said that I know what the Lord wants me to do; I wasn't quite sure of it myself, but after listening to what she had to say, I was hoping that she could tell me and then I would be on target with pursuing it.

She spoke about me having creativity and using words to express things; she asked me to send her one of my writings. I paused for a moment when she said *"my writings."* Then, I read to her a poem titled *"Mercy on Me."* She listened intently before expressing words of praise and how God inscribed His handwriting on my heart to write the words from heaven. I felt comfortable to tell her about the book that I had started writing about my life story.

Some time had passed. Then, while I was sleeping one night, God showed me in a dream several pages of cursive writings. I could vividly see the words, but I couldn't remember what they meant. Also, I began writing inspirational poems by the hundreds. The Holy Spirit would wake me during the night and give me the title to the next poem; most times I would write while lying in bed with the moon light guiding my fingers. I kept a pen and paper close to me; I would write at work, the doctor's office, and everywhere that I went. I was astounded by the experience.

There was a glow on my face that I couldn't conceal. People would stop me to ask about it, and I would tell them, *"It's God and His Holy Spirit."* It was a spiritual transformation that happened to me; it opened my eyes to acknowledge that there was a calling on my life. I was no longer in denial about it from that point on. I developed a hunger and thirst in desiring to know more about the things that God was planning to do in my life, but I was afraid of not being able to pass the tests.

I believed that Prophetess Hopewell was positioned in my life by God for such a time as this. I had never met a stranger that had such a gift of prophesy and was able to speak into my life; signs and wonders followed. However, on the other side of the coin, I had to learn that a prophetic word was for a season, perhaps the present or the future, and the messenger may only be in our lives long enough to deliver the message or for a season or two. When the assignment is over, they must obey God and move onto the next assignment.

Since I did not understand that I wasn't supposed to hold on to Prophetess Hopewell and accept that her time was only a season in my life, I became a sounding board to her as she shared some of her past and how things were going in her life. I learned about her struggles and wanted to help in some way. We continued to speak over the phone, but she became more interested in my poems and would ask me to send her copies to pass out to homeless people, shelters, and the church. I realized how much she helped me in the inception process and copyright, and for that I was grateful.

She was weaving herself into my life by talking about my gift to write for the Lord and by recommending different ways of distributing my poems to prisons, charity causes, and other avenues; however, it became too much to deal with because she had crossed the line with me. I would always pray to

God and ask for guidance through the matter because I didn't fully trust her. Through much prayer, over time I was able to see the other side of her by her actions. When I had had enough, that's when the Lord gave me the strength to walk away from her.

In conclusion, Prophetess Hopewell was able to see some of the things that the Lord was planning for my future. It was obvious by her actions that she took her eyes off of God and became obsessed with my gift and where God was taking me; she wanted to remain in my life until the prophesies that God spoke were manifested. However, I remained humbled throughout the whole experience because I realized that the gift I have is not mine; it's the Lord's. He entrusted it to me and I am forever grateful.

The Lord will sometimes send us a word from a stranger; however, when the assignment is over, they must obey God and be willing to move to the next assignment. When someone speaks into our lives, it will align with the scriptures in the Bible to confirm its validity. The signs and wonders will follow the words that are spoken over us. If someone speaks a word that doesn't agree with our spirit, we are to pray about it and examine what the word of God says about it. The word that is being spoken should be to warn, exhort, and comfort us.

The Bible tells us that we are all sinners and need a Savior to save us. If we believe it and accept the truth about Christ, and repent from our sins, we will be saved. God's love and grace is bestowed upon us because of the blood covenant that Christ made for us. He is offering us a way out of the darkness so that we may walk into the light.

The Lord wants us to know Him through his word. As we learn and walk according to the word, we are like growing trees and must bear the fruit; but some of us do not believe that it's God speaking through His word, so we casually read it or aren't patient enough to remain steadfast in reading it. It may take years before a scripture or chapter gets down on the inside of us, but we must continue to read, pray, and meditate on the word for the duration of our earthly life. If we take it for granted and think that we know it well enough, it will become like a dull axe; therefore, we must always be willing to get sharpened by remaining steadfast in the word and being a student for life.

For those of us who continue to stumble and are weak, sometimes it's easy to become clingy and attached to people that we may feel safe around or that are helping us get through a tough time. When God sanctions a matter in our lives, He will remove all stumbling blocks, people, places, and things. He shares His glory with no man.

There are so many things to learn in life about the natural order of things as well as the spiritual order. The Lord is teaching us how true the word is by giving us tests according to our level of faith and knowledge of Him. We are all in different places on our journey; we have been given a measure of faith and are encouraged to read God's word to help us walk through whatever we have to face. When we get stuck in a place or part in the test, the Lord will reveal the next step to help guide us, and that is our sign to know that God is walking through it with us.

There are blessings and rewards awaiting those that are laboring and remaining steadfast in the word. Our tests are producing the fruit of the Spirit in us. The Bible tells us in Galatians 5:22: "But the fruit of the Spirit is love, joy, peace, longsuffering, kindness, goodness, faithfulness, gentleness, self-control." When the test is over, we will be graded on how well we did. As we mature spiritually, we can sometimes see how we should behave in a matter according to what the word says and how to resist following our feelings in how we should react in our pain.

When our lives start to bear spiritual fruit, the Lord is smiling down upon us. He gives us favor everywhere we go; he's opening doors that we cannot see and windows that we cannot touch. We are all God's children, and He wants the world to see His light shining within us. It's easy to pick up the Bible and confess to be a believer, but when we've gone through the fire and tests, the Holy Spirit is living and dwelling inside of us by guiding and helping us to fight the enemy and teaching us that with Christ all things are possible. We belong to the Lord, and He is faithful to fulfill every word that He has spoken over our lives.

I felt so blessed to know that my prayer list didn't get lost by the wayside. The Lord sees through us, and He knows how to draw us. I have heard many people say negative things about other people, including myself, and treat them bad, but we need to check our hearts and minds and be willing to forgive those who have hurt us. It does take time for people to turn away from their selfish desires; the majority of us may have to go through many more tests to learn about becoming selfless. The Lord does have a plan on how to shape and mold us into soft-hearted human beings.

When we get tired of fighting against what God wants for us, we will stop looking outward for our peace and happiness, and we'll start to feel how He feels when we get our prayers answered by running. When we run back to doing things our own way, it's called a one-sided relationship and we're the ones always on the receiving end. Sometimes the Lord will hold back on answering our prayers, if He knows that we are going to leave Him out of our daily lives. We cannot see how unfair and selfish it is on our part, but as we learn to wait on the answer to our prayers, the Lord is slowly changing our character into becoming more like His Son, Jesus.

How can I put it simply? We are always going to need something from the Lord; if we have enough faith to pray to Him, we should be willing to trust Him with our hearts. God is bigger than our needs, and He knows everything about us; therefore, it is an honor to know that He is our heavenly Father and has claimed us as His children through Christ Jesus.

As the Lord reveals to our hearts the things that only He knows about us, we will start to trust in Him. He wants an intimate relationship with us; we belong to Him, and He knows how to give good gifts to his children. His word tells us in Matthew 7:7-8, "Ask, and it will be given to you; seek, and you will find; knock, and it will be opened to you. For everyone who asks receives, and he who seeks finds, and to him who knocks it will be opened."

I truly believe that when our hearts are in the right place with God and we love Him, our prayers are more than a to-do list for Him. We are sending up prayers of thanks, gratitude, worship, and praise for all that He's done in our lives.

My prayers are living proof that I serve a mighty God, and He is known by the works that He does. I feel God's love as I witness the things that He's done in my life. Thus, having a prayerful life became a vital part to my relationship with the Lord. He will work out everything in our lives to show that He is worthy to be our God.

CHAPTER 6

We Pray, God Listens, then We Wait – Repentance and Redemption

God is designing a relationship with mankind through our prayers. Many of us automatically turn to prayer when we cannot see our way, nor have the answer or know the outcome of a matter. Although there are times when we may feel that we have everything under control and things appear well, in essence there is always something that we're going to need from the Lord that will require faith and putting our total trust in God's hand.

When we turn to prayer, it is the first step of faith; however, when we ask for our needs and wants first, we fail to acknowledge our gratitude by giving thanks to God. We have so many things to be thankful for: life, family, health, food, shelter, and God's love; He sent us His only begotten Son, Jesus. The word of God tells us in the book of 1 Thessalonians 5:16–17, "Rejoice always, Pray without ceasing, in everything give thanks; for this is the will of God in Christ Jesus for you." There is another part of our prayers that we must include with our petitions: let us give thanks to God for His will to be done and thank Him because He is the one answering that which our hearts need.

As we reflect on the times God brought us through something that we didn't feel was possible without Him, His track record is indeed worthy of our praise and testimony. It is the evidence why we should give Him thanks for everything. When we have these words on our lips, "the Lord will do great and mighty things," because He requires us to give Him thanks in the good times as well as in the bad times in our lives.

When we reach the point of allowing God to be Master over our lives; our hearts will soften to feel what He is saying through the word. We are commanded in the book of Psalms 37:4, "Delight yourself also in the Lord, And He shall give you the desires of your heart." The Lord already knows what we need, and He is willing to bless us more than we know. His word is there to teach us what He wants from us; in order to know Him and live in agreement with His will, we must get to know Him by building a relationship.

We are free to love, worship, and fellowship with God at any time. Some of us may feel unworthy or too unclean to feel welcomed to talk to Him and serve Him in some capacity because of our sins and our lack of faith. However, His Son, Jesus, died and took our punishment and made atonement for our sins with His Father. We are living today under grace because Christ lives. He settled our sin debt in full by restoring our relationship with the Father. We cannot earn grace; it is unearned, undeserved, and unmerited divine assistance through the saving power of the blood of Jesus.

Therefore, we must pray and seek God for ourselves and desire a relationship with His Son, Jesus. The work of the cross is the everlasting blood covenant that binds us to Christ and God forever throughout eternity; those who believe in Jesus have this abiding faith and are rooted in knowing how our sins were forgiven by accepting His resurrection and all that He did to recompense our sins to His Father.

Sometimes, we are easily turned away from thinking that God wants to use us for any good. Many of us have been taught to believe that we are not going to amount to anything, because of our parents, the past, weaknesses, flaws, and character defects. We were made by God, and there is purpose for our short comings; the word tells us in the book of 2 Corinthians 12:9, "And He said to me, 'My grace is sufficient for you, for My strength is made perfect in weakness.'" Therefore, we must learn what the word says, so we will come to know what Jesus died for and accept everything He is offering to us.

The Lord is doing a work in our hearts daily by allowing us to feel pain, cry, have compassion for others experiencing trials, and He is pointing us in the right direction to follow His will and plan for our lives. It's easy to say, "I don't believe it," only because we haven't a clue how much God loves us. The good and the bad that happens in our lives are the signs and road markers indicating to us where we should turn to follow the path that was predestined for us.

We must continue to let go of the anger and seek forgiveness by asking God to take all the hurt and negative feelings away from us. Any relationship would be difficult to enjoy when the other person is in turmoil and hurting. It would be hard to open our heart to love a person without having to feel their hurt, pain, and negative energy. It would deplete our joy and kill the desire of having something special and meaningful in our lives.

Think about how much harder it would be to surround ourselves around people that don't want to forgive, have anger problems, and are always harping on the bad things that they've experienced. Sometimes, we act this way because of the suffering, pain, hurt, setbacks, hardships, and calamities that happened to us. We don't have to live in the past, or continue to carry the baggage into new relationships, because the Lord sees us as we are and knows what shape we're in before we make that imperative step to start a new relationship with Him.

The heart holds the issues of life; eventually the things that we are feeling or harboring will start to flow out of our mouths and show in our behavior. We have to stop running from ourselves, and the pain, disappointments, and hurt. There is someone greater than all of life's difficulties and troubles; His name is Jesus.

Well, with Jesus being our personal friend, companion, and savior, we can trust what His Father's word tells us in the book of John 15:3:8 "You are already clean because of the word which I have spoken to you. Abide in Me, and I in you. As the branch cannot bear fruit of itself, unless it abides in the vine, neither can you, unless you abide in Me. I am the vine, you are the branches. He who abides in Me, and I in him, bears much fruit; for without Me you can do nothing. If anyone does not abide in Me, he is cast out as a branch and is withered; and they gather them and throw them into the fire, and they are burned. If you abide in Me, and My words abide in you, you will ask what you desire, and it shall be done for you. By this My Father is glorified, that you bear much fruit; so you will be My disciples."

As we turn to Jesus for our salvation and trust Him to be all that His Father tells us that He is, He will draw close to our hearts and create in us a new spirit so that we will be new creatures in Him. He loves us enough to smear us with His aroma by removing all of the ugliness that resides within us and wash us with His blood. We will become yoked with Him and sin will no longer enslave us in bondage.

He makes us desirable to be the light in the world. This process is amazing and supernatural. It's compared to a baby being born; when we become born again, Christ changes our spirit and heart to follow Him. We yearn to know Him and are sensitive to obeying His Father's word and the Holy Spirit. Our discernment of spiritual things will start to become stronger as our eyes and ears become opened to the truth about God's word.

Many of us have been awakened by the Holy Spirit to listen to the word of God by studying the Holy Bible, praying, and going to church. The word will grow inside our spirits to help us live daily according to the instructions in the word. When the enemy sees this happening, he will send all kinds of distractions to persuade us to lose interest. We must confess with our mouths and believe in our hearts that Jesus loves us and has proven it by His death and resurrection.

Therefore, we must take the necessary steps to keep our minds renewed through the word. Seeking a relationship with Jesus is vital in knowing Him and learning what is required to building an intimate relationship. Thus, we know that in having a relationship both parties have needs that must be met, in order to feel secure and have trust.

The word of God speaks to our hearts about the things that God wants to teach us; it exhibits His behavior and character among exuding His power and Spirit to the world. As we desire to love and are willing to live in the light, the Lord will reveal to us through the word how to walk and abide in His word daily.

As our hearts are softening, Jesus will show us how to surrender our selfish desires in exchange for His Father's will. The things that we thought were significant will start to diminish as our desire for sinful things fade away.

It takes time to have this mindset that the word teaches us to pray for. The way life seems today, no one can precisely know what tomorrow holds for them, but Jesus. He holds today and tomorrow in His hands, and there's no greater time than today to sit and dine with Him.

During the first phase of getting to know Jesus, I could attest to how the blessings were pouring into my life and the times when I couldn't go any further on my own. He was carrying me through the darkness that was plaguing my soul. The Lord is precious and mighty are His works. He is worthy of all the wonderful things that are written about Him and witnessed by the righteous.

There is great power in speaking the name "Jesus" aloud; it permeates throughout the heavens and earth, piercing the soul and spirit of man. The angels are ready to obey His command before dispatching to earth. He is called faithful and wonderful; when I needed a friend and someone to protect me from danger, He showed up and manifested what the word tells us in the book of Romans 8:33: "Who shall bring a charge against God's elect? It is God who justifies. Who is he who condemns? It is Christ who died, and furthermore is also risen, who is even at the right hand of God, who also makes intercession for us. Who shall separate us from the love of Christ? Shall tribulation, or distress, or persecution, or famine, or nakedness, or peril, or sword?"

When I lift up my head to look towards heaven, my soul is at peace in knowing that Jesus cares about His people. As I trust the word to guide me, I am able to witness how the word transforms a person. Also, as I remain steadfast in studying the word, I pray to become the person that God predestined in Christ.

The attacks that I went through helped me to recognize the spiritual warfare that Satan was using to destroy me, but God was using these experiences to teach me the word and to call upon the name of Jesus. I would sit and cry at times about how powerful God was in rescuing me from the enemy's grip.

I cannot express enough how important it is to read and learn the word of God. If it were not for the word, I know that I could not have made it through my times in the darkness and the snares that I overcame. I recognized that I needed Jesus, but I also needed His Father's word to arm myself with power. The more that I prayed and cried out to Jesus, His Father was pruning me so that I would bear fruit. If I say that I know Him, where is the evidence of it? I am humble to witness that the word is working and abiding in my life.

No matter how much we know, we still do not know enough to stop laboring in the word. We are jars of clay and are always being placed on the potter's wheel for repairs, in addition to being transformed into the image of the Son of God. No one jar is quite the same; the Lord knows how much work each jar needs in order to be useful for His glory.

The closer I got to Jesus, I wasn't easily led astray by every whim of distraction nor by what I thought I needed and wanted. I was able to recognize Satan's plots and schemes that were in my path. When the word started increasing inside me, I was able to apply it to different situations that I came across. As I recalled the scriptures that I used, I could see the power of the word and the fruit in my life.

As time moved on I was able to see how much the Lord was walking with me. I would write Him letters about how I felt concerning the things that I liked and disliked, in a humble manner. I was uncertain if He would get upset with me, but I learned early that He already knows everything that's in our hearts.

This time I could feel that I didn't want to disappoint the Lord; I had been diligent in listening, writing, praying, and running from evil. I wanted to be kept by Jesus so tightly, because He was fighting all of my battles.

At times, things were out of my control. I had no idea how to help myself when I was living in despair. I remember the time when I got a new boss at work that didn't care for me. I felt intimidated and feared losing my job to some degree. I continued to watch how the enemy was using him to make me feel anxious.

Since I knew how to perform my duties, I did everything that I could to stay out of his way. I prayed to God to give me favor with the new boss or to take me off of the job. One day while I was at work, my boss awarded me with a gift certificate for my work. I was surprised by it and continued to do my work to the best of my ability.

Several months later, things had changed with the way the boss treated me. He went back to speaking harshly and made the work atmosphere hostile at times. He requested that I stop working overtime. I knew that it was time to pray by the tone in his voice and the abruptness.

I felt as though I was being bullied because he was snooping around my desk and nitpicking my work. He didn't understand the company's policy and protocol that well, but wanted to reprimand me about the things that he felt were inconsistencies. I remember telling the Lord that I wasn't going to quit anymore jobs, and if the company wanted to fire me, then they would have to do it. My heart was heavy and I was exhausted by trying to follow along with the office politics. I felt at that point that there was nothing left for me to do, because I was exhausted with trying to prove my value.

I remember waking slowly the next morning, and I faintly heard, "Denise, remain humble." The tone and the words sounded as a command; I knew immediately that it was from God. I pulled myself together by quieting my mind so that I could ponder on humility.

When God speaks, there is no need to say anything but to obey. I was amazed at how He was concerned about the details in my life. I realized that God was present in every situation, whether big or small. I got into the habit of praying, and when I called upon Him to help me, there were signs and wonders that followed my prayers.

In conclusion, I ended up leaving the company. The Lord opened a door for me to walk through. It was a lonely and unfamiliar path to tread, but I crossed that bridge. I trusted God and walked across it by faith and believed that He didn't bring me this far to leave me. He did make a way of escape and provision for me to get through that difficult time.

Every trial, victory, and battle that I experienced catapulted my prayer life. I walked through the fire and the waters to get to the other side, where God was leading me. He is able and capable of performing His word in our lives.

When we feel free to talk to the Lord about everything, it becomes easier to consult Him about things before we respond to matters. Sometimes, we can make a big mess or a mountain out of a mole hill. If it had not been for God speaking to my spirit by telling me to remain humble, there was no question in my mind about how things could have turned out and it certainly would not have worked out in my favor; all I can say is that there is a God. I can testify that God can handle anything and everything that concerns His people.

However, we must be willing to know Him, and the only way for it to be of our free will is through a relationship. We have a choice in the matter, whether we feel that God is worthy of our time and love. If we wait or delay in choosing Christ tomorrow, it may be too late; just remember that He's present right there in your car, bedroom, office, home, hospital, sick bed, and prison. If we could open our hearts to give Him a chance, sincerely things will all work out for our good.

Sometimes, it's hard to believe what someone else thinks or believes, but God is no respecter of a person. When we pray, God listens, and then we wait. The process may take time, because the Lord is doing a work within us as well. He's teaching us how to remain steadfast with our thanksgiving, faith, prayers, and seeking Him by performing His word and supernatural works in our lives.

We all have heard that God may not be there when we want Him to be, but He's always on time. Whenever the Lord shows up, we must be ready to receive and know that it is by faith that we will continue to persevere. Sometimes when we receive an answered prayer that we've waited long for, we tend to feel more grateful and humbled and are willing to testify to others about the process and for what God did because it's not easy to forget something that cost us something. Most importantly, we will remember who helped us get through our struggles and trust God because He heard our prayers.

Many of us have to be pruned by the Lord to sharpen the word in us. Sometimes, the wait is part of the process to our answered prayers because we tend to remember the scriptures when we apply the word to our problems, issues, situations, circumstances, prayers, and faith. The effective part of the word is when we see the fruit being manifested in our lives as we triumph through the hard times the most.

There are times when we may feel that God requires so much from us in order to reap what He is offering to us through His Son, Jesus. However, it's human nature to feel that way, because we cannot simply please God enough in our own strength and ability the way that we are. Once we are born again with help from the Holy Spirit, we will become conquers through Christ who strengthens us.

As we continue to seek the Lord's righteousness we are being conformed into the image of His Son. The more that we yield to the Holy Spirit's guidance we will have more victories in our earthly matters. He will let us know how we're doing according to our obedience and walk with the Lord. He will continue to chase after us by keeping us shielded and protected from the enemy's enticements. The things that used to make us run away from God's plan and will for our lives will no longer have a grip on us. Our eyes will become open to seeing things that are not of God, and the Holy Spirit will show us the way to go. We must continue to follow and trust in God's plan for what's best for us. We have no idea what the next step is when the Lord is leading us until He reveals it. Therefore, we must remain close and steadfast to our faith in Jesus.

When we are weary, anxious, or in trouble, Jesus has the power to give our souls rest from all of life's heavy burdens. He offers us His yoke because it is easy and His burden is light. By having a relationship with Jesus, we are able to rest in knowing that He is the risen savior because He's right there in the midst working things out for us.

His works are not hidden; we must be willing to read the word to know for ourselves how great He is. As we continue to have our own experiences and journey, please keep in mind, in order to win the race we have to participate and cross over the finish line.

CHAPTER 7

The Fruit of Prayer – Salvation and Worship

*W*hen we are able to perceive our prayers being manifested in our lives, it's an amazing feeling to know how good God is. He continues to work everything out for the good of those that love Him. His word is written to teach us how we must relate to Him and to harness our faith.

The work that He is doing in our lives is still in process as we learn to fight the good fight of faith. When we get into a consecrated place in our minds and hearts and recount the things that God has done for us and His people, God is saying that He is able to do even more than what we could ask or think according to His Spirit that works within us.

A lot of times in our flesh we feel fear, discouragement, and doubt when things are coming against us; but when we have a relationship with the Lord, it becomes distinctly natural for us to turn to Him for the help that we need. Only He can strategize a plan at the last minute and win the battle without any human hands. We must remember that He is a great God and is there in our time of need, trouble, and victory.

Many of us panic at the thought of trouble, but if we would read the word before the chaos breaks out into our lives, we would know that we have an advocate named Jesus fighting on our behalf to draw us close to His Father's will. The Bible tells us in 2 Chronicles chapter 20 about King Jehoshaphat's enemies surrounding him in battle to destroy him and God's people. The Lord defeated his enemies before their eyes. He did a supernatural work right there in the midst of the battle before the people. He's doing the same mighty work today; only those who are growing in the spirit are able to discern these miracles. If we would be still and allow God to whisper into our ears, hearts, minds, spirit, or dreams, then He will begin directing our steps every day.

The Lord is saying that He wants to answer our prayers and use us for a consecrated life of prayer. He knows that there are certain people who are willing to obey Him and be His messengers to deliver His word, adding nothing to it, and taking no word from it. Many of us are calling upon Him, but don't really know Him, or know who we are in Christ. He already knows us and knows if we desire to know Him.

The people that God chose to use in the Bible weren't perfect people— He didn't have any favoritism—but He saw their heart and the love in them towards Him by not taking any credit or the glory from Him during their victories over their enemies. When they called upon Him, immediately signs and wonders followed them and their prayers were answered.

Praying to know Him and praying from my soul has to come from the heart, mind, soul and spirit. He wants this for each of us as we yield to a life of prayer. As many of us have experienced, when we're in trouble, we immediately look for someone to intercede for us to reach God, so we can feel safe about having our prayers delivered. Some of us may feel that it is the pastor's, priest's, or church's responsibility to communicate on their behalf to the Lord.

However, we can no longer continue to lean on other people to talk to the Father for us; Jesus died so that we could have a relationship with Him. There are no obstacles, phone lines, buildings to travel to in order to talk to God about anything at any time.

Sometimes, we might need to say a fast prayer and we need to know that we can do it. He is present and His arms are outstretched towards us. No matter what our sins are or how impure we may feel, we must still try to humble ourselves and come to Jesus because our sin will always cause us to feel dirty and keeps us separated from knowing God; further, it could cause us to miss out on His forgiveness and salvation and building a relationship with Jesus.

When we pray for others and start to see our prayers being answered, we are motivated to partake in rejoicing, because we have witnessed the power of God moving in their lives. The blessings of answered prayers cannot be compared to any material thing, because money cannot move nor persuade God. Someone needs your mouthpiece to say a prayer for them. We have no idea how the Lord wants to use us, but we should be willing vessels.

I didn't know that I could come to the altar and sincerely tell God how I felt about the issues and troubles in my life without feeling afraid. Jesus removed the veil, so I could make my way to the altar. I remember humbly walking down to the altar, even though my heart was so full of rage, doubt, and hurt. The Lord began to comfort my spirit by telling me if I read His word I would understand more about how He operates and moves in matters.

He is willing to always bless us as long as we give Him the glory and refrain from seeking the spotlight and making alliances with the wicked. The Lord is working through our weaknesses and desires to reward those who seek Him diligently. We are not alone when we don't understand how we're going to come out of a situation beyond our control or power. The greatest weapon is speaking the word of God and coming humbly to Him in prayer.

The Bible tells us that there's power and life in the tongue, so we must learn to use our mouths and speak the words of faith to decree those things that be not as though they were. The Lord began to reveal to me how victories have come through the fruit of prayer: healings, being persistent until justice was won, favor when I turned to the left and the right, taking the steps of faith, protection from my enemies, and discovering my purpose.

The time that I've spent praying has multiplied a magnitude of blessings in my life. I can attest to it because the Lord has been a way maker. I was downsized and let go from work around four years ago; I didn't know how my situation was going to work out. I remember praying fervently during the next thirty days about a clear vision and how to proceed from there.

I didn't disclose my concerns and fears about my situation to my fiancé, because I didn't want him to feel sorry or obligated to take care of me. I was persistent with talking to the Lord daily, and because I had grown close to Him, it was natural for me to pour out my heart to Him. Sometimes, when I couldn't fall asleep at night I would replay the prayers that I taped and ponder how God had either answered one of my prayers or how He was moving me along my journey.

The Lord had answered my prayer when He spoke to my fiancé to marry me. We got married six weeks after I lost my job. I was blessed with more by stepping out on faith. I went from being independent to unemployed to depending on God fully. When I surrendered to God to marry my husband, Thomas, in His time, that's when things started prospering in my life supernaturally.

During my time off work I attended the Illinois State Sexual Assault & Domestic Violence Advocacy Training, became an ordained minister, author, and co-founder of a non-profit. I was in awe of seeing the things that I had prayed for come true.

Since I couldn't fathom in my finite mind how the Lord was going to bring any of these things to pass, I prayed for clarity and direction. I made the necessary steps that it took by faith to get there. It was a divine work step by step to walk, because I was afraid and clueless on how to do any of these things on my own.

The Lord walks with us daily when we revere Him and humble our hearts. It becomes personal when you desire to love and please the Lord with your life. He has done so many great and wonderful things for me, and there is nothing better that gives me the assurance that I am loved and His child.

I have grown to understand that I have been given a responsibility to help build the Kingdom of God. My wisdom, knowledge, and experiences are being passed on to help others get through the difficult times in their lives. Naturally, I don't feel qualified if I had to be compared by the standards of this world, but it's quite obvious that God searches the minds and hearts of men to discern whom He should chasten, send, and exalt.

If I had listened to what people were saying about me when I was lost, I never would have made it through. It was God almighty arranging everything in the background. He closed my ears from hearing the noise from this world and removed the people, places, and things that were hindering my walk and commanded that I follow His path.

The times when I would see other people worshipping the Lord I didn't quite understand it or trust if it was real. But now that I have witnessed the supernatural hand of God upon me, I find myself bowing my head while pondering how sweet God is and allowing my tears to flow freely. He is worthy to be honored and worshipped, and I am willing to be vulnerable. He holds a power that causes all things to bow and worship Him, whether it is good or bad.

The best gift to share with someone is telling them about what Jesus has done for you. Many times, we are hesitant about letting someone know that we love Jesus, because some people tend to say mean things: we must be a Jesus freak, we are trying to convert them, or that we're religious. It's not the case when you have been touched by His Spirit; you know that you've been blessed in such a divine way, and the glow that the Lord smears on you permeates when you smile and it attracts others. Sometimes, they can't resist asking you about your smile.

While we're praying to God for the answers to our prayers, we will have many experiences that will either draw us near or pull us away from God. Everything is set according to His divine plan for our course. In the book of Joshua 1:5, the Bible tells us, "I will not leave you nor forsake you." Sometimes, we don't feel so confident in what the word says or know how to apply it to our lives, until we're tested.

When the dark times and storms come, we are reminded of the scriptures in the Holy Bible to remain steadfast in the Lord with all of our mind, strength, soul, and heart on what we have read and learned about God's word. Although, we will know for certain if we trust God during the test. But certainly, as we carry our own cross, we must not forget that we are disciples following Jesus, and we're going to have to go through something and give up many things in order to be all that we are called to be as His followers.

The Lord is manifesting His blessings in the earth as we lift up our praises to Him daily. Some of the fruit of our reward is being bestowed upon us through our dreams. He's given us the power to change our circumstances and the ability to serve Him in a greater way. When we are transformed into a new creation, He removes all of the stains and blemishes of the past, so we can move forward into the newness of His everlasting love.

Our cup does run over when we have so many new concepts about becoming an entrepreneur, identifying our life's purpose, doing missions abroad or locally in our communities as God continues to open doors that we cannot see and windows that we cannot touch. We are no longer fighting the same old battles anymore. The Lord has destroyed the yoke of bondage off of our lives when we surrender to accepting His yoke. Our new dreams have been given divine inspiration through the Holy Spirit. The obstacles of the past are no longer pressing on us to turn back; it is absolutely an incredible season to be in after laboring and sowing prayers.

We will become consciously aware of knowing that God is our captain as we praise Him from our hearts and remain steadfast in His word; there is so much more that the Lord has in store for us. The blessings of the Lord continues to harvest seeds of His goodness into our lives through the things that we touch, speak His word over, and pray about as we remain humble servants.

As we open our hearts about the goodness we've received and our experiences as overcomers, we are now vessels being used for the work of the Lord. We know that the word is working, because we're being transformed by allowing our minds to be renewed daily. It's liberating to see the power and splendor of the living word being formed in us through faith in Christ, Jesus.

We must live our lives as though we are expecting Jesus to come dine with us at any time of the hour. He is the vine and we are the branches; our hearts should always remain pliable. We will never know fully the next test that's ahead waiting; therefore, we must remain connected to the vine. As we exhibit love and patience for one another, we are bearing His fruit.

The evidence of bearing good fruit in our lives indicates that the seed was sown on good soil. When I was going through my hardships, I had to hold on to the word to pull me through. As I learned how to decree it into my own life, it began to manifest its power. The word is life, and when we decree the word, we are speaking life to a thing, situation, or person. When we pray to God for something, all things are possible if we believe.

We know that God hears us when we pray, because He continues to clothe us and provide shelter and food. Sometimes, we take these things for granted, until we have very little or anything left. He always sends us an angel in many forms to answer our prayers.

We all have stories about our lives and how we feel regarding our struggles and agony; if you are still going through, please don't give up. There is a harvest to be gathered in the reaping season. The Lord is on time, and He's present in the time of help. He desires for all of His children to pray to Him. There's nothing too hard for God; truly He reigns.

When our seeds bloom, they have the ability to keep reproducing from generation to the next generation. Therefore, we must always be mindful of how we're sowing into the lives of others. We are striving to be conformed into the image of God's Son, so we will continue to bear fruit of the characteristics of Christ.

CHAPTER 8

A Harvest of Prayers – Evangelism

Wile the word is being sown into us through prayer, reading the scriptures, and meditating on them, we are being prepared for a harvest. When the time comes to gather what has been sown, the harvest will produce the seeds and fruit of our prayers.

We have been given a purpose to fulfill during our lifetime along with different tests and lessons to learn. We are clueless to this purpose and divine plan, because we are naturally incline to conform to this world system of doing things. It seems to be the way of life to follow along with how everyone else is making a living and by following the world in how to become somebody.

As we strive to learn something from each test and lesson, our seeds will bloom. Sometimes all we can see is negativity when we don't understand a matter, but God has a way of using it to bless us or by turning bad things around to give Him the glory. He has placed people on our path to touch, bless, and inspire us to believe in ourselves and to have faith.

As a mighty warrior, we need to start believing that we are a part of Christ's family and these are the weapons that we need in order to overcome our circumstances. The seeds of hope, faith, and trust have been planted into our souls and spirits. When we are asked about our faith, hope, and trust in God, sometimes it may stir things up within us, thus causing us to examine ourselves to affirm whether we still have the desire to be loved and blessed.

We must continue to do our best, because we are carrying the seeds of our future within us. The concept of sowing may bring forth a field of flowers or weeds, but when we become a part of the process, we take part in what we desire to receive through our prayers and faith. We have the power to decide what we are hoping to reap. Our minds hold the thoughts that we think about ourselves, others, and God.

Learning to be selfless is a part of the process; we must pray for others to be blessed and loved, too. When we have experienced how God answers prayer, it causes us to believe for others as well. This, too, is a form of sowing: praying for God's best over someone else's life, thus causing a harvest in our own.

When we discover that our words are forming the things we speak, we will not hesitate to talk to God and give Him the glory from our lips. He has given us the power to believe in ourselves and to connect with Him through our prayers.

We have been given God's grace through Jesus, a new life where we are able to believe that all things are possible through Him. The time is now to start living this new life that He died for; we need to read the word to learn what we've inherited.

As believers, many of the blessings that we are hoping for have already been given to us: God's love, eternal life, and the forgiveness for our sins. These things may seem far from our sight, but knowing that we have a home with God in heaven affirms why we must trust in Him.

Meanwhile, our prayers are being answered. Whether small or large, a one-minute-long or hour-long prayer, we must still have the hope that we will receive it. We cannot take the credit for anything when we receive His blessings. But of course, we do play our part when we apply our faith and hope. Our Father in Heaven is revealing how much He loves us by imparting to us His grace and favor, knowledge and wisdom, all while we're being conformed to the image of His Son.

When we are elevated to see beyond our finite minds, our passion and drive becomes exhilarating, because we have tapped into the supernatural. It is God's grace directing us toward Him for the plan that He has predestined for us.

Someone is praying for us while we are trying to get through our struggles. We may never know who it is; the Lord has prayer warriors and angels assigned to help assist in our spiritual and natural growth. When we sit down to say our prayers, we have the same opportunity to pray for someone other than the people we know: the homeless man or woman, cab driver, police officer, or orphans. It is necessary to show our smile and kindness, because it lets someone else know that there's still hope in the world.

As the Lord reveals to us how much He loves us, we will learn to rest in Him. The process does take time; although we want the harvest now, we must be patient until our season comes. The journey has a lot of twists, turns, and many stops along the way. While we learn to love people that need love, we are getting closer to knowing God. It's not easy to show love to a stranger, someone hurting, mean, or that has a hygiene issue, but it is possible to show them love when it resides within us. Our love can be in the form of a smile, kindness, or pointing them in the right direction to get some help for their situation.

Many of us still have a difficult time showing love and forgiveness, but until we learn that forgiveness is also a commandment, we can expect to be placed back onto the potter's wheel. We will learn to obey what God commands from us when we stop making excuses as to why we should or shouldn't forgive. We have been forgiven for our sins when Jesus obeyed His Father's will to die for us. He didn't go back and forth about the matter. Indeed, it was a ransom price that He paid to forgive us for our sins, and He tells us in His Father's word how we must learn to forgive others as well. It's not a choice about whether we feel that the person is deserving of forgiveness, because it is a commandment. Remember, we were sinners trespassing and separated from God through our ignorance and sins.

It isn't easy to love, forgive, and walk in God's word, but we must try daily to make a step. We need our hearts to be ready and open to obey Him. Someone is in need of forgiveness while laying on their sick bed. It would truly mean the world to them to hear the words of forgiveness before they close their eyes for the last time. As we pray to the Lord, He will give us the strength to hold on while He brings it to pass.

We are connected to God when we realize that the air we breathe is His. Our mind tells us that He's someplace far away, but He's as close to us as our mouths and hearts. We must whisper praise and offer Him thanks for waking us daily. We must direct our thoughts and motives towards being servants.

The walk does get lonely at times, because we will have to give up things that we aren't ready to let go. Our friends and family will act out at times, or start to pull away; however, it will not all make sense. We don't have the option of picking who will be by our side as we continue the quest. When we reach a place of refuge and peace, we will know that it is God's rest.

During the times when we question God, we need to humbly come to Him in prayer. He is there and ready to comfort our hearts and give us the peace that surpasses our understanding. We were called by God to step forward to live a holy life for Him. The challenges of moving on and forward is a part of the divine plan to teach us to continually pray.

As we start to trust that the Lord is by our side, we will let go of thinking that we need to know everything or be in charge of our lives. The spiritual work is being done within us to help us obey God when He says, "I will never leave you, nor forsake you." The word of God tells us in the book of Hebrews 4:12, "For the word of God is living and powerful, and sharper than any two-edge sword, piercing, even to the division of soul and spirit, and of joints and marrow, and is a discerner of the thoughts and intents of the heart." The word along with the power of prayer and our faith are insurmountable when we apply them.

We must recognized that God's Holy word fights for us to become conquerors in Christ, Jesus. We cannot believe parts of the scripture when it seems fitting to us or our situation. We must declare the works of the Lord and memorize the word, hiding it in our hearts. It is the source to connecting us to God and a lifeline to knowing Him.

Remember, we are seeking to know who God is for ourselves. The word of God tells us in the book of Hebrews 11:6, "But without faith it is impossible to please Him, For he who comes to God must believe that He is, and that He is a rewarder of those who diligently seek Him." There is no turning back, because our steps have been erased. The word of God is a lamp to our feet and a light to our paths.

The majority of us have been taught at an early age to treat others as we would like to be treated. However, many of us have different values and morals that we follow. As believers, we are all servants of God and are given commandments for our learning and instruction. Thus, the word of God tells us in Romans 13:9, "You shall love your neighbor as yourself. Love does no harm to a neighbor; therefore love is the fulfillment of the law."

The commandments may seem difficult to follow at times, especially when we allow our mind and sight to dictate how we should treat people. We cannot rely on our feelings, because our flesh is insensitive to the word of God. We are blind by sin, and our flesh has a sinful nature. The word is teaching us how to walk in love, the truth, and wisdom as we continue to study and apply scripture to our lives. Regardless of our feelings and what we see on the outside of a person, we are supposed to follow Christ. The seed that we receive and plant will be the seed that produces the harvest.

Our Father, God, desires for us to love Him and to love our neighbor, family, friend, and all mankind. He is love and the utmost expression of it, and because of His love, we are able to feel loved when we build a relationship with His Son, Jesus. He teaches us in the Bible that "love is the fulfillment of the law." When we fall short in keeping the commandments, He continues to love us by giving us His grace. Therefore, we must walk in love and be ready to befriend the lonely and help those who are in need or troubled.

The Bible tells us in the book of 1 John 2:3, "Now by this we know that we know Him, if we keep His commandments. He who says, 'I know Him,' and does not keep His commandments, is a liar, and the truth is not in him. But whoever keeps His word, truly the love of God is perfected in him. By this we know that we are in Him. He who says he abides in Him ought himself also to walk just as He walked."

We must pursue prayer while we're waiting to be filled with the Holy Spirit; He is our guide, helper, and protector. When we see our brother or sister stumbling in the word, we must intercede for them. There is not one who doesn't stumble in the word, because we are still in our flesh on this side of heaven. The flesh is always at war with the spirit.

Acknowledging our faults and sins to the Lord allows Him to help us with our weaknesses and teach us about repentance. We must be active participants in the race and be willing to accept chastening. When we attempt to make the same mistakes, the Holy Spirit quickens our spirit by helping us to listen and to remember the word of God before we act.

We seem to hold fast to the seed that we've sown after our disobedience and our convictions, longsuffering, and chastening. There is a time for correction "thus says the Lord" and consequences to our actions. It is His will that we learn much through the things that we suffer. Of course, it doesn't sound nice to us when we have to endure longsuffering, but it will help us to become better Christians. We will become spiritually conscious to accept knowing that longsuffering is a part of the fruit of the Spirit.

When we receive God's correction, we must be willing to accept it, because there will be a harvest if we continue to bear fruit. There will be a time to gather what has been sown, thirty, sixty, and a hundredfold. When the word of God is rooted within our hearts, it continues to manifest good fruit into our lives, thus causing an overflow that comes by being connected to the vine in Christ, Jesus.

CHAPTER 9

The Prayers that Heaven Answered – Acceptance and Alter Call

As I speak about how good God is to me, it is a part of my praise and worship to give Him honor. There were many days and nights and years and seasons that passed by before I was able to perceive the essence of God's power working in me and through my circumstances.

When I learned about who I was in Christ and my identity, I became spiritually conscious of what the Bible tells us in the book of Matthew 7:7–8, "Ask, and it will be given to you; seek, and you will find; knock, and it will be opened to you. For everyone who asks receives, and he who seeks finds, and to him who knocks it will be opened." As believers, we have been given promises by God, and He is willing to honor His word.

There are so many of us who confess that we believe in Jesus and what the Bible teaches, but when we examine our lives, we need to be able to effectively tell others about how we have been blessed according to the word of God. We must remain students of the word in order to gain the understanding of what God has promised us through His Son, Jesus.

When we learn how to pray God's word over our lives, the enemy becomes powerless and surrenders to the word. We are loved by the almighty God, and He shows no partiality towards any man. We must be willing to remain consistent with our prayers, and when the Lord blesses us, we must be determined to walk with Him.

The relationship process is ongoing and will continue as long as we are willing to love, obey, and listen to the Holy Spirit. It is certainly an intimacy that develops between us when we become sensitive in hearing, obeying, and learning from the Lord. Many of us may feel as though we cannot hear anything from God, but that isn't true because He is always speaking to us through His word when we read it.

When I was a little girl around the age of seven, my mother and stepfather had an alcohol addiction. Their drinking was excessive and out of control, because they would fight after becoming intoxicated. One particular evening, my brother and I were outside playing in front of our home and I remembered hearing my mother yelling and screaming while running out the front door. She jumped inside the car and yelled for me and my brother to get inside the car. I became startled as I opened the passenger door and jumped inside; as I looked towards the front of our house my stepfather was aiming a machine gun at us. I ducked down in my seat after seeing the fire from the bullets coming straight at us.

We got away that night and made it to safety. The car was hit with eight bullets on the passenger's door. I examined the holes where the bullets entered, and I couldn't understand how I survived without being injured or struck by a bullet.

Subsequently, there was another shooting that happened late one evening. My brothers and I were trembling in fear while we waited quietly upstairs in my brother's bedroom. We heard our mother screaming and yelling for me to come to her. I panicked as my body became paralyzed, because the fear was overwhelming. While calling for me again, I heard my mother running and falling down the stairs. I remember my eldest brother holding the Bible in his hands and telling us that if it wasn't our time to die God would protect us.

When he unlocked the bedroom door, I slowly got up and started walking towards my mother. When I got to the top of the stairs, she screamed as I got closer. Suddenly, she grabbed me and put me in front of her. While we were screaming at the top of our lungs, my stepfather aimed his machine gun at us and started firing shots. The bullets ricochet into the ceiling above us.

As I reminisce, it was the love that God had for me that spared my life. As a little girl, I remember crying and sobbing with great fear, because I didn't want my life to end tragically. Today, I know in my heart that it was God that saved me. I didn't know His Son, Jesus, nor about Him dying for my sins. He gave up His life for me, so I could have a new life with Him. I have learned that our steps are ordered by the Lord, and you must believe it too.

Since those days, there have been many hills and mountains to climb. Through my prayer life and journey with the Lord, He has been a mother, father, friend, companion, healer, and deliverer. His presence is obvious in my life. I can talk about Him, because I called and cried for His help many times, and He answered me. The grace that covers my soul draws me closer to knowing that He lives.

He will pick us up when we fall down; we must not be afraid to step out on faith. Everyone's faith is given to him by a measure, so let it be unto him that believes all things are possible, if you believe. It's amazing to feel the goodness of God's love. It would be a shame if I had missed out on knowing what He is able to do in my life. The reverence of serving God is knowing His Spirit and trusting Him to be the only one that can make me whole.

There is no one that cares so much about our healing when we are sick and bedridden but God. The doctors are there to do their job, and when they've done all that they can do, they prescribe more medication, and that's when we get the final report. The scripture tells us in the book of Isaiah 53:5, "But He was wounded for our transgressions, He was bruised for our iniquities; The chastisement for our peace was upon Him, And by His stripes we are healed."

As believers, we must continue to speak the word and pray the word over our bodies and for others. We must remain active in seeking our healing. The doctor's report isn't final; don't give up on God, because that's when He is able to turn it around for His glory.

When the abundance of God's goodness overtakes us, our cups will surely run over with mercy and goodness. The things that we cannot see with our physical eyes are a part of the spirit realm. We must take hold of believing that God wants us to experience Him and be able to relate to His love. Our minds and hearts can become filled with the distractions of the world, thwarting us from allowing Him to make an entrance into our lives.

When our praises are released from our lips, hearts, and spirit, the windows of heaven are open to pour us miracles and blessings. Sometimes, we may feel the presence of God when we start to release our tears, anxieties, worries, and fears. We must lift our voices to say thank you and not hesitate because we're doing it for an audience of one—which is God.

As we carry the word with love, our light dispels the darkness and negativity that surrounds us. The opportunities that we come across are the platforms to sharing what we've learned about Jesus. His light follows us wherever we may go to exude hope to a dying world.

During my late twenties, I was experiencing one setback after another. I was struggling with work, finances, and coping with discrimination in my field. Things began to spiral out of control in my life when I received more bad news about my first marriage. It struck my heart deeply to the point that I attempted suicide.

I vividly remembered the day when I had confronted the issue that was bothering me. My anger turned into rage. I ran into the bathroom with a glass of alcohol and found some prescription medicine and pain killers. I swallowed the pills along with drinking the alcohol.

As my body started slowing down, I decided to take a nap hoping that I would feel better when I woke up. However, I wasn't thinking clearly that this could possibly be the last time that I would be alive. While I laid there, images of my life were racing through my mind. As I closed my eyelids, they would not stay shut, and since my body would not allow me to fall asleep, I reached for my daily word to read. I decided to call the number on the back of the devotion pamphlet for prayer.

I felt compelled to call my friend because I couldn't sleep. While we were talking, she immediately detected that there was something wrong by how my speech was slurring. I confessed that I had taken some pills, and she screamed in my ear and begged me to put my husband on the phone. She asked him to take me to the hospital right away. We both were in a confused state of mind, because of the arguing and alcohol use, and by God's grace, we did make it there.

The recovery process was long and dreary. I went through bouts of depression and felt ashamed of my actions for trying to take my own life. Apparently,

I was in a broken place emotionally and mentally, and I carried the broken pieces with me. My mind was tormented by the thoughts, agony of hurt, and love that I still had for my husband. I prayed as I cried out to God for help, but I didn't feel close to Him nor did I believe that He was listening to me or my prayers because things had gotten worse.

As I reflect on the matter, God was there because I made it through. I would have had liver failure if I had not made it to the hospital in time to have my stomach pumped within an hour. Nonetheless, the damage and stress that I put my body through could have been detrimental. When we are hit by surprise with something disturbing, it transmits the information to our brains fast; if we cannot regain composure to calm ourselves down, it could put us in a tailspin leading us to do something dangerous.

During that time the prayers that I had prayed were answered; the Lord had blessed me to find a better job that appreciated me. He did send me some sunshine at the right time to help me regain the strength that I needed to keep on living. My soul was seeking refuge, peace, and a new direction in life. Although I was married, I realized that I had to seek God for my change and healing.

Sometimes, we need an emotional and mental healing so that we can let the past go and move forward. The milestones that I had encountered revealed that God was carrying me the whole time. Every day I felt compelled to read something inspirational and uplifting to feed my spirit with hope. The material that I read seemed to reference God or a scripture in the Bible. Although I didn't turn to the Bible often for the answers, God was still directing me to turn to Him for my help. I never gave up on having faith, because it challenged me to do something.

The Lord was bringing me through these hard times to make me stronger and to become a soldier in His army. He was revealing His Spirit and love each time I would hit the bottom. When we hit a wall a few times, it will certainly wake us up and cause us to watch and learn how to go around it.

I am consciously mindful that I owe God something because He carried me. I attribute a part of my desire to help people in need to my grandfather, because he set values and morals in my life while I watched how he loved his neighbors. He was a compassionate Christian man who became a bishop, and he'd travel from North to South crossing many paths and meeting people from different walks. He was reaching the lost by serving and feeding them. He didn't hesitate to ask someone if they were saved and tell them about Jesus.

When I discovered that I shared my grandfather's passion to help people, I knew that there was something special and different about me. My journey has been hard, but through it all, it did not deter me nor change what's in my heart. When we learn to listen to our heart and use discernment concerning people in need, we should be mindful that it may be God's way of revealing to us our purpose.

My words of gratitude are for all the things that God has done for me in my life. While I still have breath in my body and am able to share and inspire others, I am committed to the call and work that He has predestined for me. The doors that He opened for me to speak about my journey, I have learned to walk through by faith and trust that God will always be with me.

When I became a born-again Christian, I knew that something different was taking place within me. I prayed for God to fill me with His spirit, because I wanted to know Him for myself. I needed His power to be present in my life whenever I called on Him.

While my life was being transitioned to a spiritual calling, the Lord was revealing to me through my dreams that I would preach His word. I had several dreams that prepared me to step out on faith to trust and believe God. The day did come when I preached my first sermon titled "Live as You Are Called." The whole experience felt like a supernatural birth; while I was speaking, the Lord increased His spirit through me and took over my voice and spoke to His people. My heart was overflowing by the time I released the message; the tears flowed from my eyes because I felt His power.

It was very humbling and fearful for me; I felt inadequate and afraid to go before the Saints. I prayed for God to take over and asked that His will be done. As I reflect back on my former years, I was wandering around in the dark, blinded by sin's enticements. I would have never made it through nor would my eyes have opened if it wasn't for the goodness of God's grace.

The blessings and triumphs that I have experienced with God's help soften my heart to sing praises about Him. His word teaches us how to walk circumspectly. He covers the righteous under His shadow and gives rest to the weary. He is with us no matter how hard the road may seem; we must pray daily to receive revelation knowledge while reading the Bible.

We cannot comprehend the word fully through our intellect because of our finite ability to understand the knowledge and wisdom of God. The word gives life, and the Bible tells us that it is living and powerful; it created the things that we now see in the natural as well as those things that exist in the supernatural and those things to come.

As believers, when we accept Christ Jesus as our Lord and Savior, the Holy Spirit comes to dwell within us to help teach us the word of God so that we will learn to obey and be able to retain it, as He enables us to remember the word of God during the times when we are in need of instruction, direction, protection, and when we call upon the name of the Lord Jesus. The word is our daily bread that feeds our souls and spirit, so we can remain spiritually alive and connected to Christ. There is no other substitute; the Holy Spirit is the greatest teacher, sent by God and Jesus to witness, and He is the Spirit of truth, whom we can fully depend on and trust to keep us close to Christ. In John 15:26, we read, "But when the Helper comes, whom I shall send to you from the Father, the Spirit of truth who proceeds from the Father, He will testify of Me."

The Lord is shaping and molding His word in us at all times. We may not believe that something is happening when we measure ourselves to the world's standards. When the Lord steps in to do a work, He doesn't go by the world system, our exterior, guidelines, or text books. His processes for preparing us are completely different and just. Therefore, we must wake up and not faint when things don't go our way, because God has another plan.

As believers, we have a part in what happens to us by consciously filtering what comes out of our mouths, because the Bible tells us about our thoughts and tongue; Proverbs 18:21 tells us, "Death and life are in the power of the tongue, And those who love it will eat its fruit."

The Lord was moving mighty in mine and my husband's life during the year 2013. My husband received a prophecy on January 4th while he was on Facebook. I remember writing it down because the person had instant messaged him. As things began to move for us in the natural and supernatural, it was very evident what the prophet had spoken to my husband: "the release was on in 2013."

We had been praying for a relocation out of state but were unsure where to go. The Lord had impressed upon our hearts for two years that we were going to move and that our ministry was not in Illinois. When I started fasting, the Lord began to show me new dreams about how He was going to use me. He often shows me things in my dreams, but this time it was frequent visions regarding our prayers for the relocation. The Lord was preparing my heart to get ready and to cooperate with my husband during our move. I remember He instructed me to not get on Facebook, and I took a sabbatical from it. I continued to study the word and prayed with my husband consistently and waited for the Lord to guide us through every step.

My husband put in a request to relocate through his work. Subsequently, we received our confirmation to move to Georgia. The Lord put on our hearts to solely rely on Him for this entire move. We prayed daily for strength and clarity. The harder things got, the more I cried. There were so many decisions to be made, and we had no idea how to get started with the first step.

The people that we needed where divinely sent to us. We sold our home in three weeks, and a new grandbaby was born the same weekend we got two offers on the house. Things were hectic and we still didn't have a place to live in Georgia. We made our visit over a five-day span, and it still wasn't looking good for us. It was very hard to press through everything because we needed some encouragement. It can be very hard sometimes to find people that are encouraging and bold speaking about their faith. The main thing that we had to remember was that we had God's approval in this matter, and that was the most important part. My friends did offer to help me with the packing, but I didn't have things sorted out well enough to decide on what was going or staying. I did appreciate their support and generosity for offering to help.

There were so many distractions and things to do. I was emotionally unprepared, and things took a toll on me. Sometimes, when you're stepping out of the boat on faith as Peter did, you have no choice but to focus on Jesus and pray that He really is there to catch you when you fall. We didn't quite know how to put this move together to make it go smoothly, and it was unclear to us how we would actually complete it.

The Lord touched my ex-husband's heart to offer his help with driving the U-Haul truck and with arranging the help loading and unloading on both ends of our move. My youngest son helped me with the driving, and the eldest gave us some financial support. It was a blessing to us, because the Lord was revealing how He can bring a family together in peace and love to fulfill what He has ordained. We love them and are forever grateful and thankful for their love and help and for everyone else that showed us support.

The plan that God had in place made it possible for us to know that He was working everything out for our good. There was no way that we could have done it alone. He provided the help, resources, and finances that we needed to cover our expenses. We prayed and He answered us. The glory belongs to the Lord almighty. He gave us strength when we were weak and the courage to keep walking. We knew that our families and friends had many questions about our decision to move to Georgia, and they didn't understand why we moved so quickly; but when God spoke to our hearts, we made up our minds to follow Him and kept our focus and eyes on Him at all times. We believed that our move was a divine blessing by God, because he put this whole thing together and He did not fail us.

During the move, Thomas was in Seminary for his Masters of Arts Christian Ministry. It was extremely more than he could handle all at once: a full-time job, planning an out-of-state move, supporting a daughter having a baby, along with selling a home. The Holy Spirit covered his mind through all the chaos so that he could complete all of his studies and blessed him to receive his Master's Degree from Seminary. It was indeed a long and tedious process to balance among work and family life.

It is quite obvious how God moved in my life through my prayers. I would have never known how much He loved me without going through the danger, testing, suffering, hurt, and pain. He was leading and directing every detail of what I would have to endure to reach the place of dwelling in His presence. We learn obedience through the things that we suffer.

We will never get to know who God is until we take the time to learn of Him through His word. He is a Spirit whom we cannot see with our natural eyes, nor touch with our hands. The book of John 4:24 tells us, "God is Spirit, and those who worship Him must worship in spirit and truth." We must learn to pray to Him and surrender to read His word. If we only knew how much power we could have by knowing God's word and submitting our time and obedience in learning who Jesus is, we could experience many breakthroughs by declaring God's word over our situation and lives.

The journey is spiritual and we must be willing to humble ourselves and accept God for being a Spirit. As we move along our path, we will learn to value prayer, because it connects us to heaven. The power that is being released when we speak God's word provides the answers to our prayers, the healing that we need, the help to prosper in health and all things that bring God the glory. It also shields us from danger seen and unseen as we walk along our paths. Satan will flee from us when we use the word to rebuke him. Therefore, we must get the word down on the inside of us in order to know how to fight the enemy.

Sometimes, when we try to explain to others about our conversion with the Lord, they don't know how to receive it or show any compassion; but we can chose to look at it one way. It's hard to interpret and perceive spiritual things to the natural man versus a born-again believer. It doesn't make sense to someone that doesn't study the Bible or have any knowledge of who Jesus is or all together who has rejected Christ. We need to pray for others to accept Christ and share the good news of the gospel to everyone that is willing to listen.

The Holy Spirit is working all the time in our lives to help us surrender and yield to our Savior's command. As long as we hold true to accepting Jesus as Lord and Savior and telling our testimony, the Holy Spirit will live in us to perform the good work in us that God predestined and continue with the regenerative process of making us born-again believers.

Therefore, we can read and rest our minds on the promises found in the Bible in Ephesians 1:3–12: "Blessed be the God and Father of our Lord Jesus Christ, who has blessed us with every spiritual blessing in the heavenly places in Christ, just as He chose us in Him before the foundation of the world, that we should be holy and without blame before Him in love, having predestined us to adoption as sons by Jesus Christ to Himself, according to the good pleasure of His will, to the praise of the glory of His grace, by which He made us accepted in the Beloved. In Him we have redemption through His blood, the forgiveness of sins, according to the riches of His grace which He made to abound toward us in all wisdom and prudence, having made known to us the mystery of His will, according to His good pleasure which He purposed in Himself, that in the dispensation of the fullness of the times He might gather together in one all things in Christ, both which are in heaven and which are on earth—in Him. In Him also we have obtained an inheritance, being predestined according to the purpose of Him who works all things according to the counsel of His will, that we who first trusted in Christ should be to the praise of His glory."

Our testimony is never too old; we must never stop giving Him the glory. Indeed, the path that God has for us to walk is the one that will draw us closer to Him. It may seem hard and difficult at times, but know that God sees our beginning and end. He wants us to know that He loves us by allowing us to go through things in life as He reveals Himself through His word. The fruit of His love continues to show us mercy, as we learn to obey and wait for Him to bless us. He makes us rich by renewing our minds daily with the word and sending us new mercies.

I have witnessed how it feels to be loved and protected by our heavenly Father; death passed by me. I no longer fear dying; and no matter what happens in my life, I will be raised with the Lord. I gained something that was worth every setback, tear, loss, and suffering: a relationship with Jesus.

CHAPTER 10

The Overflow From a Prayerful Life

My heart was filled with an unquenchable joy as I talked about my Savior. There were not enough words within my vocabulary to be explicit enough. His compassion and mercy captures the heart when we long to know Him. The Spirit of the Lord searches the innermost parts of our being to reveal how deep we are connected to Him.

I needed time to stand still while I surrendered to the presence of the Lord; He was shining the light of peace and hope upon me. The feeling of knowing how blessed I was completely overflowed into all areas of my life. I was conscious of how I walked, talked, and treated people. I was in awe of how real God was in my life. It wasn't just with words; He was allowing my heart to fall in love with Him. The way the Lord handles us is unbelievable; tongues must confess and knees will bow.

There is a grace that covers all of our sins which overflows and opens the doors of our hearts to help us accept Jesus as Lord and Savior of our lives. There is no place on earth to find the Lord; we must recognize within our minds and hearts that the Lord is omnipotent, omniscient, and omnipresent. His power, knowledge, and presence resides within us; we must seek to know Him to awaken our subconscious.

When we're in the storm, it seems impossible to know whether we will make it out safely. The hardest part is not knowing when the storm will be over. The one thing that is certain is that we are the righteous of God through Christ Jesus. The Lord never sleeps nor slumbers and His eyes are on the weak, humble, and righteous.

Many people are familiar with their own pain, and they don't understand how to let go of some things and let God work in their lives. We toss and turn, because we're too afraid to step out on faith and the enemy is using our pride and fears to fight us and attack our minds. The greatest battlefield is in the mind, and once we allow the lies and evil to set up camp, we will experience spiritual warfare.

The Bible tells us in the book of Ephesians 6:14–18, "Stand therefore, having girded your waist truth, having put on the breast plate of righteousness, and having shod your feet with the preparation of the gospel of peace; above all, taking the shielded of faith with darts of the wicked one. And take the helmet of salvation, and the sword of the Spirit, which is the word of God; praying always with all prayer and supplication in the Spirit, being watchful to this end with all perseverance and supplication for all the saints." Therefore, we must learn through the word how to put on the whole armor of God. In essence, the Lord is our truth, peace, shield of faith, deliverer, victor, so therefore, we must not faint, because the battle is not ours for it is the Lords'.

As we share the gospel with the world, we need to be mindful that someone is always watching us to see how we are living our lives. The fruit that we show them will either draw others to Christ or repel them. The word tells us in the book of Galatians Chapter 5:22-23, "The fruit of the Spirit is love, joy, peace, longsuffering, patience, goodness, faithfulness, gentleness and self-control."

When we are faced with situations, problems, dilemmas, and circumstances in life, it will exhibit what kind of fruit is within us by the way we react. The world may not understand why we choose to love someone that has hurt or abused us, have joy in the midst of our trials or peace when we don't know what to do when our lives are turned upside down; the Holy Spirit is teaching us what the Father's will is for us and nurturing our hearts and minds to become one in Christ through the word. Everyone is human and capable of making mistakes; no one is perfect, and that's why we need a Savior to rescue us from the penalty of sin. The Lord is revealing to us that we must have a contrite heart and turn to Him for repentance when we sin.

While our souls rest from the various trials of life, we will learn to be patient and wait on the Lord to renew us. He is using us to draw our family, friends, and others to Him. We can see the hand of God touching our loved ones by turning them around from a life of sin, healing those who have been sick, giving His people second chances, and helping them to find their way back to Him.

The work of the cross allows us to turn to Jesus for the forgiveness of our sins. He exchanges His righteousness for our sins when we accept Him as our personal Lord and savior. The Bible tells us in the book of Matthew 26:27, "Then he took the cup, gave thanks and offered it to them, saying, 'Drink from it, all of you. This is my blood of the covenant, which is poured out for many for the forgiveness of sins.'" The power of the blood seals us to the new covenant that He has with His Father to offer us salvation and everlasting life.

The outpouring of His blood was poured upon many, thus compelling us to believe by faith that Jesus is the risen savior and Messiah. His love is overflowing upon us when we bow to His Father's word, Spirit, and love. We have the assurance that we are loved and saved when we accept Christ and become born again through the working power of the Holy Spirit.

As we mature as saints, we must stand firm on the word, because our foundation is the cornerstone that the builders rejected—Christ. We are part of the rock that the Lord, Jesus, is forming by gathering each stone to build His church. Therefore, we must be willing to get up from sitting on the pews at church and show the world that Christ lives in us by meeting a need in someone's life. It will go a long way, because what touches the heart reaches the heart.

We must desire to allow God to work in us; He is doing a work in others and performing His word daily. Our prayers must move beyond asking for material things; fervent prayers must come from our hearts as we continue to trust Him and allow His will to be done.

The blessings of the Lord do make us rich, because He adds new mercies and benefits to us daily as we continue to give Him glory and praise for all that He's doing. He has the power to take our worries and cast them upon Him and fill our minds with His word, love, and praise.

When the Lord blesses your life, there is nothing that anyone can do to reverse it. There are people that we may have been in relations with that probably have thought evil or been jealous, envious, angry, or have conspired to do mean things against us at one time or another. However, there is no one that can curse what God has blessed. The Bible tells us in the book of Numbers 12, "And God said to Balaam, 'You shall not go with them; you shall not curse the people, for they are blessed.' So, it would be senseless to fight against what God has blessed.

As I reflect on the time I had visited a psychic, I remember she told me that a woman had put a curse on me. I didn't know what to think or how to react, because I couldn't think of anyone that I had caused harm to do such an evil thing. She had promised that she could help me remove the curse, if I was willing to pay her for the services, and guaranteed that she would be able to tell me the woman's name who did it. Subsequently, on my second visit, she did not give me their name, but only two letters in the name.

I've had numerous friendships in my lifetime that ended not so well, and I've learned that it was not God's will to continue being friends with many, because we were on different paths; their season was over. There was no way that I would have been able to figure out who could have paid someone to put a curse on me. Also, during those days in my depression and confused state of mind, a prophet told me that a woman sent a suicide spirit to me.

Therefore, I moved on past the thought of being cursed, because I knew that God loved me; He sent Jesus to die for my sins, and I believed in Him enough to protect me from the evil one. Since the weapons formed against me did not prosper, I continued to press towards seeking the Kingdom of God. I did pray and repent for my sins and for being tempted to opening the doors of darkness. I had to depend on my faith and prayers, because darkness was all around me.

Although I didn't know my Bible well enough to know what God was declaring about my life, I prayed and called on the name of Jesus to deliver me. I knew that there was power in the name of Jesus, and that was taught to me in my former years. Since maturing in the word, there is a scripture in the book of Proverbs 18:10: "The name of the Lord is a strong tower; The righteous run to it and are safe." As I meditate on it, there is no one that assures me that I can run to them for the safety that I need when I'm going through a spiritual battle but Jesus.

Therefore, I proclaimed the promises of God's word over my life. In Psalms 118:17, we read, "I shall not die, but live, And declare the works of the Lord." As our cups run over with knowing how good God is and how much He loves us, we will take the time to worship, pray, read the word, and give Him the glory. There is no other way of knowing Him but through spending time alone, dwelling in His presence and studying what He is trying to teach us through the word.

Today, I rejoice because if it had not been for the Lord on my side, the path I was on could have destroyed me. He brought me out of being foolish, thinking wrong thoughts about myself and others, and being brainwashed by the trickery of Satan. The Bible tells us in the book of Jeremiah 29:11, 'For I know the plans I have for you,' declares the Lord, 'plans to prosper you and not to harm you, plans to give you hope and a future.' God will continue to prove to us that His word is living and powerful by working it into every situation and matter that concerns us. When we fall in love with the peace that we have in knowing that He's able to care for us better than ourselves, it releases a joyful praise from our souls as we learn to obey and follow the path that He is revealing to us.

Jesus is teaching us to trust that He will be with us wherever we go until we are united with Him. As believers, we must remember that there is a season for everything under heaven, and if we hold on to our faith and the word of God, He will restore everything and give us double for our troubles. We will go through testing but think it not strange. The testing of our faith will produce patience in us, thus allowing Christ to reign over our lives.

When we're going through these battles in life, sometimes our money, intellect, and influence cannot bring us out of it. It requires the power of God and our faith in Christ Jesus to reveal to our spirits, minds, and hearts that we are more than conquerors. His Holy Spirit comforts us while filling us with a peace that we cannot fathom nor explain.

As conquerors, we will become mighty warriors and soldiers while fighting against Satan and his imps. Everyone that believes in the Lord Jesus will endure suffering and persecution for having the faith in the risen Savior. Saints, it is all a part of drinking of the cup and eating the bread that gives us eternal life.

We cannot live by "bread alone; but by every word that proceeds from the mouth of God." Therefore, we must study the word which is the Holy Bible in order to understand how to discern spiritual matters, relate to God, obey Him, and to keep His commandments. The material things in the world are temporal; we must pursue Jesus. He is our advocate. He is petitioning on our behalf the prayers that we pray; it is by His Fathers' mercy and grace that we have the scriptures and the Holy Spirit to help us hold on.

We no longer have to toil about how our problems are going to work out, because it's already done. We need to trust God, continue our relationship by giving Him glory, and obey what the word has taught us.

When we fall into various trials, we need to turn to Jesus first for the help that we need, and through His Father's divine will, things will start to come into alignment in our mind, thoughts, and faith regarding the help and answers to our circumstances. He is all that we need to give us the victory in everything. Thus by giving us His life in exchange for our lives, we can totally depend on Him and the word for everlasting life.

Sometimes, we may feel disappointed when things don't go the way that we had anticipated, but we must realize that there is a reason, and perhaps the Lord may have something else better. Since the Lord sees what we cannot see, we must talk to Him about how we feel, but we should never allow our feelings to grow hard towards Him. Remember, there are no coincidences when we belong to Christ. He knows everything about us, and our steps are ordered.

The adversary will use the closest person to plant a seed of negativity into our minds about our faith in Christ. Remember, our minds must be renewed daily through the word of God in order to recognize when the enemy is devising an attack against us.

I wanted to protect myself from getting hurt, but I never wanted to stop helping people. I asked the Lord to give me discernment so that I would be able to avoid the unnecessary troubles that I had put myself through in the past. He did it for me; I feel blessed in knowing that He was willing and able to teach me how to adhere to His wisdom.

When we ask for things with a pure heart and our motives are godly, it is likely that the Lord will give it to us. The Bible tells us in the book of James 1:5, "If any of you lacks wisdom, let him ask of God, who give to all liberally and without reproach, and it will be given to him. But let him ask in faith, with no doubting, for he who doubts is like a wave of the sea driven and tossed by the wind." Thus, our hearts must be open to receive and ready to obey the Holy Spirit as we yield to the Lord's command.

The power belongs to Him; there is nothing too hard for the great "I AM" to do for the righteous. Every prayer that heaven answers, we must be mindful to give thanks and remain humble in the Lord. Our lives should be an open book; we are living epistles and disciples of the Lord Jesus Christ.

The desires that we have may not always be with the right motives or be good for us. The Father desires for us is to love Him with all our mind, heart, soul, and strength; therefore, He will continue to help us get to the place where we are able to have a mind like His Son, Jesus, and we must be willing to let go of anything that keeps us from maturing into spirit-filled people of God through praying to know Him. Many of us will experience a spiritual purging; the word and Holy Spirit will work together to cleanse our minds, hearts, souls, and spirits. We will know the difference, because our lives and desires will change as the Lord fills us with the fullness of joy found in Christ Jesus.

The Lord wants to bless us with more than our spiritual cup can hold. The overflow must be poured out until it impacts others to believe in the goodness and mercies of the Lord. When we are blessed, it follows us wherever we go, and the favor of the Lord connects us to God's riches and blessings. As people of God, we must put our total trust in Him to draw us close and to rain His glory upon us in due season.

CHAPTER II

Prayer Transcends across All Boundaries

*T*here are many nations within the globe. We have many distinct traits which separate us in this diverse world. Our various cultures, arts, foods, races, religions, laws, and languages divide us from the perception of living in a world united in peace. Additionally, there are some common threads that we share: our blood is red; we feel sorrow when someone we love passes away, loneliness, hunger for food, thirst for water, and the desire to be loved.

Also, there are many borders that people cross over to find their dreams. The different laws and customs that govern each country are upheld by the governing officials and guards daily. Therefore, certain and legal conditions must be met before getting a passport to leave a country and entering another country.

Unfortunately, the wealth and natural resources are not distributed evenly throughout the world. Thus, many people seek better living conditions elsewhere. Many of us are forced to leave our homelands in search of the dream to live in peace and to become enriched with the bare necessities.

As we discover the complexities of living from day to day, many have experienced cruelty in some form or another by being enslaved through their oppressors, beaten, killed, and stripped of their possessions by another race.

Evil is running rampant throughout the world globally every day: wars, hate crimes, bombings, assaults, human trafficking, drugs, and senseless slayings.

Many are seeking refuge from such atrocities, whether it comes in the form of asylum, migrating to a new country, establishing roots, change, work, etc. Sometimes the conditions that we live in may cause us to feel empty inside, poor, desolate, and helpless. There are many forms of the struggle that could end up knocking on our door.

Sometimes there's barely enough bread to eat; in other words, there are no scraps to put together. The medicine supply is limited in certain places, because there are no practicing physicians or clinics to provide healthcare to the people. When there's an epidemic or a serious illness that falls upon a person, many obstacles may need to be triumphed before getting access to the medication that will help in aiding and saving lives. The hospital could be many miles away, perhaps in another country; the injured may not be strong enough to travel; or they may lack money or proper documentation to access the resources. As a result, many lives are lost through the struggles of pursuing the dream to a better life.

The countries that continue to strive towards industrialism, capitalism, communism, and trade are in competition to gain wealth, power, and world recognition. As we become integrated through the internet, technology, politics, and science, we are impacted by these influences and the powers that be, because we share or are in need of some of the resources to live. People are living day to day, and some are hardly getting by because of the systems that are in place concerning the rich, middle class, and the poor. As life gets harder for most, there's not much left but to turn to our faith and spirituality.

We seem to no longer make worship, praise, and fellowship to God a priority, because we are too busy trying to find a living and obtain some economic wealth as well. We have become as completely numb as zombies to how God feels when we are drawn daily to connect to social media and become engaged with activities that consume our minds and the majority of our time.

We tend to burn ourselves out physically by exerting our energy and time with chasing outward things. Some of us only have little desire to pursue any intimacy with God, and that's all we have left to give.

However, when we love the Lord, we will not allow earthly things to take up all of our time. We will pursue our purpose and desire to give God the glory for our failures, successes, and victories. When we seek the Kingdom of God first, all of His righteousness will be added to us. Our joy and peace will become abundant, and our lives will become enriched with knowing that we have a reward waiting for us in heaven. These blessings cannot be forfeited if we follow Jesus with all of our heart, mind, soul, and strength. No matter what we go through, He is just and faithful to perform His word in our lives.

When we open our eyes to gaze at our surroundings, we must trust that there is a God that put everything in its place to accomplish what He purposed it to do. When we surrender to His will, our hearts will become open to thinking and believing.

When we are born into poverty, sometimes our minds are conditioned to think that way. It may be difficult to imagine hope or grasp the faith to believe that there's another way out. As we take a deep breath, there is hope through our prayers. The process to getting started begins with our words and thoughts. We must be willing to create the opportunities to attain the life that we want by envisioning ourselves living it.

We are placed into different circumstances and situations to help us develop faith, perseverance, patience, tenacity, resilience, and character. We are more inclined to pray when we cannot see our way out of a situation. As we make it from day to day, we tend to find the hope and strength that we need to pull us through.

Many of us have chosen to follow a church, synagogue, mosque, or the beliefs of our ancestors, because they were passed down to us. When we are new coming into the faith, we are given a list of rules to follow and are required to remain committed throughout our entire lives. We learn to practice what to say, pledge, give our tithes and offerings, serve and fellowship with the other congregants weekly. As it appears, we look united, but let the truth be told, many of us are dying on the inside. We have gotten bored with the hymns, songs, and church because they are predictable. Behind closed doors, many of us are struggling to break free from the mundane routine of just living; our hearts are yearning to experience an intimacy of love that is not tangible.

Many of us do not feel anything when we come together to worship God and may have doubts about what we believe, but we're too afraid to talk about it.

However, the Bible tells us in the book of Jeremiah 24:7, "Then I will give them a heart to know Me, that I am the Lord; and they shall be My people, and I will be their God, for they shall return to Me with their whole heart." The Lord wants to fill us with His love, and Holy Spirit so that our hearts will turn to Him as we grow to understand that our bodies are a living sacrifice, holy, and acceptable to God.

The reason many people are wavering and have become bored with going to church is because they want to experience God for themselves. He no longer dwells in temples made by hands; He is ready to make His presence known within us when we learn to obey Him by keeping our bodies free from sin, because sin separates us and defiles us in His sight.

The word of God is free to all, and blessed are those that hunger and thirst after His righteousness, for they shall be filled. There is more to life than just trying to survive and following a religion that has a long list of rules that we must follow in order to feel close to God. It is hopeless to allow ourselves to be placed back under bondage by trying to follow the law, because no one was able to keep the whole law without breaking at least one of them in the Old Testament.

The Bible tells us in the New Testament, book of James 2:10, "For whoever shall keep the whole law, and yet stumble in one point, he is guilty of all." The scriptures in Romans 3:21–26 tells us, "But now the righteousness of God apart from the law is revealed, being witnessed by the Law and the Prophets, even the righteousness of God, through faith in Jesus Christ, to all and on all who believe. For there is no difference; for all have sinned and fall short of the glory of God, being justified freely by His grace through the redemption that is in Christ Jesus, whom God set forth as a propitiation by His blood, through faith, to demonstrate His righteousness, because in His forbearance God had passed over the sins that were previously committed, to demonstrate at the present time His righteousness, that He might be just and the justifier of the one who has faith in Jesus."

According to the New Testament, we are saved by grace through our faith in Christ Jesus. There is no one that is perfect enough to keep every rule, commit no sin, nor stumble in the word, except Jesus. God sent His only begotten Son, Jesus, to die for our sins so that we could be forgiven for our sins and have an intimate relationship with Him and not a religion.

Many people fall into the enemy's trap by trying to fill the empty void that's within through a spirit of pride, stubbornness, lust, evil, alcohol, drugs, painkillers, and sexual immorality. Somehow the hole seems to be expanding the more we feed it with those things. As we become a part of the vicious cycle of feeding the flesh with the pleasures of sin, we will never be able to break free. It is hard to hide the life that we have lived in sin, because we end up wearing it on our faces. It could wind up decaying and destroying many people, because these are strongholds and the enemy will do everything in its power to strip us of our beauty by sucking the life out of us while keeping us trapped in bondage.

If we are connected to someone who is battling an addiction of some sort, as believers, it is our duty to pray for those who are in need. There are people all over the world seeking prayer, crying during the night for relief, and enduring hardships that may cost them their lives.

When we come together in agreement on behalf of someone's prayer request, the prayer lines to heaven are never busy. The Bible tells us in the book of Matthew 18:19-20, "Again I say to you that if two of you agree on earth concerning anything that they ask, it will be done for them by My Father in heaven. For where two or three are gathered together in My name, I am there in the midst of them." As believers, we have the power through the word to declare what it says and to speak blessings over the lives of people all over the world.

The Lord is ready and willing to perform miracles when we live our lives in honor of Him and by putting our faith and trust in Him. The effectual prayers of a righteous man avail much; we must not allow any social barriers, creed, race, and color to hinder us from praying. He allows the rain to fall on the just as well as the unjust; therefore, we must allow Him to use us for His glory. When we consecrate our minds and hearts, the noise of this world will become mute as the Holy Spirit discerns to our spirit what we must say and do.

There are people seeking answers to their prayers; we must be mindful that we may be the only Bible that someone sees, so we need to be prepared to speak a word as we pray for them.

We don't have to travel to China, Africa, England, Poland, or other nations. We live in a diverse country where our borders have been enlarged to reach people from different walks in our neighborhoods. It is likely that we will meet people from various countries as we go about our day-to-day activities.

It is never easy to witness or pray for people when we cross paths. There are so many thoughts that may run through our minds about how to approach someone without offending them and fearing that we may end up being rejected, or feeling ashamed of our faith in Jesus.

Sometimes, when we meet people and they take notice of the way we dress, our hair style, mannerisms, jewelry, and accent, it opens the door for a conversation, and that's when we need to show ourselves friendly. The opportunity to witness may not naturally happen at the moment, but we still have the chance to smile, exhibit kindness, and ask their name to remember them when we say our prayers.

I've learned to pray for people in passing while I run errands; while at the doctor's office, dentist, or grocery store; while holding the door open for someone to enter a building; while on social media. It doesn't matter that they're homeless, pushing a cart, smoking a cigarette, even sadness may appear on their faces. I am asking God to bless, protect, and save them. This method is effective, because we don't have to know them before we say a prayer, as long as we have a heart to intercede to our heavenly Father because He is omniscient.

The way that we approach each other with our beliefs and faith has caused many to run and become guarded, because our delivery or our message was probably too pushy or condemning. We are apprehensive about religious matters because of the many faiths and atheists in the world. We are strangers to each other trying to co-exist in peace. Therefore, we must be cognitive of others by exuding love, compassion, respect, and a smile. We can learn a lot when we exhibit patience and kindness before we try to tell someone about our faith.

Remember, the seed must be planted first and then watered before it blooms. Many people are rooted in their beliefs and faith, and change doesn't happen through casual contact; it starts within the heart because it holds the secrets and issues of life. We serve a mighty God that moves past the walls we put up, the barriers and borders that we create from harboring un-forgiveness, hate, pain, ignorance, and fear. God's power transcends the natural and spiritual realms; there are no boundaries nor barriers that He cannot get through, nor race, creed, law, religion, doctrine, and there is no organization that can prevent the Holy Spirit from regenerating, renewing, and restoring a man to Christ.

The majority of people have been conditioned to follow traditions, rules, doctrines, and their religion. As a result, if we only follow religion, we would not be able to relate to who Jesus is personally, nor witness and testify effectively why we believe. Jesus does not want us to become burdened by feeling guilty because we are not able to live up to the religious demands that are placed upon us; He promises us that if we accept His yoke which is easy our burdens will be light. Therefore, we must pursue a relationship with Christ, because He is the only one that can save us.

When we proclaim Christ as our Lord and Savior and repent from our sins, we must be baptized, and the promise of eternal life begins as we follow Jesus. We must be active in our seeking, following, and belief about Christ.

We must start a new life with prayer by talking to Jesus about everything and desiring to know who He is as we read and study the word of God. The word tells us in the book of Colossians 1:15–22, "He is the image of the invisible God, the firstborn over all creation. For by Him all things were created that are in heaven and that are on earth, visible and invisible, whether thrones or dominions or principalities or powers. All things were created through Him and for Him. And He is before all things, and in Him all things consist. And He is the head of the body, the church, who is the beginning, the firstborn from the dead, that in all things He may have the preeminence. For it pleased the Father that in Him all the fullness should dwell, and by Him to reconcile all things to Himself, by Him, whether things on earth or things in heaven, having made peace through the blood of His cross."

The clock is ticking as we grow from being infants and babes to maturing in the word of God. Our lives aren't instantly changed to living a prosperous, peaceful, and blissful life, but we are always changing as we yield to the Holy Spirit. The good news is that we are now adopted into the Kingdom of God by the blood of Jesus to be called sons and daughters of the living God.

The Bible tells us in the book of Galatians 3:26, "For you are all sons of God through faith in Christ Jesus. For as many of you as were baptized into

Christ have put on Christ. There is neither Jew nor Greek, there is neither slave nor free, there is neither male nor female; for you are all one in Christ Jesus, And if you are Christ's, then you are Abraham's seed, and heirs according to the promise." As a part of being an heir to God and a joint heir of Christ's, after our baptism, the old man is buried and the new man is risen, and we are now identified with Christ's death, burial, and resurrection.

We are now a part of Christ's Kingdom and are accountable to live as His Father's word tells us to. The unresolved matters of the past must be given to Jesus so that we can move forward into the new life that He died to give us. We will never be able to do it on our own; we must pray, read the word, and ask Him to give us revelation, knowledge of what the scriptures mean and how to apply it to our daily walk.

As we continue to grow in the word, we will become seasoned as we start to settle down. We will know in our hearts that we no longer live according to our own selfish desires and are truly willing to do what Jesus would do in our encounters. His image will reflect who we are to the world. Remember, our greatest work is on our knees praying to the Father. He is merciful to us, and we must strive to show Him how grateful we are.

We are united with the promise found in the book of Galatians 3:8: "And the scripture foreseeing that God would justify the Gentiles by faith, preached the gospel to Abraham beforehand, saying, 'In you all the nations shall be blessed.' So then those who are of faith are blessed with believing Abraham." It is through love that we draw all men to Christ.

CHAPTER 12

Angels Interceding

When we turn on the television, we have become desensitized to the wars, gun violence, murders, rapes, and crimes, because we see it in movies as a drama on the screen. Society has shown us that sometimes war is inevitable before we are able to move forward as a nation. There are no guarantees when the wars will end, how many lives will be lost, or the state and the condition of the people afterward.

It doesn't seem to cease until everyone involved is either killed, injured, or a treaty is reached. We must trust that when God spares us, He will direct us to safety and find the help that we need. We must pray for the courage of our soldiers to unite in prayer when there is nothing left to do but stand.

Nevertheless, tears are shed, last words are spoken, and requests are made on behalf of legacies and heirlooms. The prayers, hopes, and dreams of our soldiers, comrades, and loved ones still remain with us. The memories that we carry with us will always be our strength to give us the hope to share our story.

Additionally, some of our greatest wars have been fought through the battle of our minds. The war doesn't end when both parties are done fighting. Sometimes, we may experience a spiritual war that involves our minds, souls, and spirit. The attacks, scars, wounds, and pain is wrenching far within us. The Bible warns us in the book of 2 Corinthians 10:3–6, "For though we walk in the flesh, we do not war according to the flesh. For the weapons of our warfare are not carnal but mighty in God for pulling down strongholds, casting down arguments and every high thing that exalts itself against the knowledge of God, bringing every thought into captivity to the obedience of Christ, and being ready to punish all disobedience when your obedience is fulfilled."

We may not be able to comprehend where God is in the midst of all the suffering and chaos that's going on around us in the world; He is crying and suffering with us as we pray to get through it. His presence is there even though it's hard to believe. He knew what suffering and pain were when His Son, Jesus, hung on the cross. When we approach God with reverence, repentance, worship, praise, and prayer, He will reveal His Spirit according to Matthew 11:26: "Even so, Father, for so it seemed good in Your sight. All things have been delivered to Me by My Father, and no one knows the Son except the Father. Nor does anyone know the Father except the Son, and the one to whom the Son wills to reveal Him."

The angels see our tears and fears; we must bow our heads and come humbly to the throne and give God our hearts. As we move forward in the midst of our pain, we may never understand why so many are dying daily at the hands and attacks of others. However, evil is rampant, and disease, famine, and poverty are at an all-time high. But we must believe that we need the Lord no matter how things turn out. God has a purpose and reason why He creates life and takes it; He cares enough to spare whom He chooses. We cannot understand why many did not survive, but we must accept that it was not God's will for them to go beyond that point. Some have been chosen by God to do a work and tell their story.

Many people have become angry at God for allowing bad things to happen. It is human nature to feel that someone is responsible for protecting the lives of the innocent. In the midst, we tend to look upward as we complain, argue, fight hate with crime, and blaspheme God when we lose our way. There is no immediate or precise answer to alleviate how the human heart feels about such atrocities and tragedies.

Satan is the spirit that entices men to become greedy for power, material wealth, money, land, and natural resources. He enters into the hearts of people who have ungodly desires and gives them the mind to possess these things. Mankind is partly the blame for the evil attacks that have been happening. The wars seem to derive when brutality is inflicted and imposed upon another race to take their power or to coerce them into becoming enslaved, or to confiscate another's land, natural resources, or wealth for one's own greed. The end result to the madness has destroyed millions of lives.

These wars are the history of civilization; we are all impacted by their negative destruction on the human race. We must understand that God doesn't look at race, social status, or our financial situation to determine if we are worthy enough to be loved. His love is powerful, and it can be felt by everyone all around the world. The atrocities can destroy the soul, but a single touch from Him can heal the mind, soul, and spirit of a man.

It is quite obvious that the times have changed and we must also. Although our cultures and world system continue to evolve, as believers, we can hold on to the immutable word of God. The Bible tells us in the book of Hebrews 13:8, "Jesus Christ is the same yesterday, today, and forever." We are assured that we can depend on the Son of God.

There are many faiths that speak about the gods; however, there is only one God: the God of the Bible. The word of God tells us in the book Exodus 3:14, "And God said to Moses, 'I AM WHO I AM.' And He said, 'Thus you shall say to the children of Israel, I AM has sent me to you.'" He desires to love those who are willing to obey Him and follow His commandments. He lights the path for His children to follow His word. The Holy Spirit teaches us how to talk, walk, live, obey, and love Him and others. He promises to bless those who walk upright before Him when their hearts and minds seek to know Him.

The angels are working day and night to perform His commands when He sends them forth. There are no interferences when God speaks; He makes the wind blow, the hail fall from the sky, the seas obey, and the wildlife inhabit their kingdom. When we are in tune with how great God is, we can see the harmony through His creation.

We have been predestined by God before the foundations of the earth were made to live according to His will. He holds the blueprint of the divine plan; it remains ambiguous until we are awakened through a life event, divine intervention, or spiritual experience. Everyone's life has a significant purpose in contributing to their community, family, cause, research, or the fulfillment of someone else's dream.

The Lord is teaching us step by step through our relationships how to pursue our calling. Some have been called to the marketplace and others to the ministry; however, we must believe that God can use us wherever we may go. The scripture in the book of Psalms 91:11 says, "For He shall give His angels charge over you, To keep you in all your ways." The Lord is never too busy, and He even affirms through the scripture that we have a guardian angel watching over us at all times.

God made us different so that we could learn how to love and communicate with each other. When we love ourselves and are kind to others, we draw likeminded people into our lives. We are likely to become more exposed to new opportunities and possibilities as we interact with people from diverse backgrounds.

When we pray to God, we must be opened minded to receive His will. Some people are closed minded when they cannot see beyond a person's skin color, religion, or plight. Sometimes, our blessing could be right in front of us, but we miss them, because we have presumed what the answer will look like or have stereotyped a person, place, or thing. We need to remember that we should be kind to all people no matter what the circumstances, because we could be entertaining an angel sent by God or miss out on our blessing.

Sometimes, we are placed into uncomfortable situations on purpose, and it is natural to want to run. However, if we are always running when things go bad, we will never learn how to trust God or develop our faith. We need to continue reading the word and mediating on it, while trusting and obeying God until we are with Him. He is orchestrating an intimate relationship with us through our ups and downs as well as teaching us to draw closer to Jesus.

Our experiences are there to teach us something new about ourselves, life, and God. When the fervent prayers of the righteous go up, heaven cries out as God charges the atmosphere and His angels to perform His word over a thing. He is able to prove that He is sovereign, even when we don't believe.

As we pray to know Him, He will reveal supernatural signs and wonders, manifestations, and His glory. There are miracles happening all over the world;

God has His arms and hands outstretched towards the righteous. When we are expecting a miracle, we need to petition our prayers to the Father and seek first His Kingdom. The blessing will come to pass by faith when we fall on our face and diligently seek to know Him.

We can be learned in many subjects in life and well versed to go beyond many borders; however, the downside of having a wealth of knowledge is when we remain closed minded about seeking God's truth. The Bible tells us in the book Matthew 11:25, "At the time Jesus answered and said, 'I thank You, Father, Lord of heaven and earth, that You have hidden these things from the wise and prudent and have revealed them to babes."

The time is now to seek to know God because He wants to be found. Many of us have been thrust into situations and circumstances that propelled our hearts to follow Him. It's not by happenstance that you survived being struck by a moving car on the expressway, robbed at gun point, won a settlement case with an incompetent lawyer, received parole from a life sentence in prison, found a matched donor when you were given only a month to live. We can say that there is a God, and it's never too late to believe in Him for your salvation and eternal life.

We may travel to different cities and countries or visit people that we feel could help us, but we must first turn to God because He holds the answer. It is important to know His will for our lives, because everything that happens to us or that we go through is sometimes permitted to prepare us for our purpose. The best way to have peace in a matter is to know and trust what God's word says about us.

Sometimes, we give up because we have been hard pressed, perplexed, persecuted, and struck down. As long as we have breath in our bodies and are in our right minds, we must know that there is something greater beyond our persecution and suffering. When we love the Lord, we can be certain that He will comfort us and bring us through it. We don't have to know what tomorrow holds, but we do need to know who holds tomorrow. The Lord is merciful, and He grants us new mercies every day. He made us to be people of faith; therefore, we must live by faith. Behold, there are new blessings, healings, breakthroughs, prophecies, dreams, and visions still to come to pass.

The Bible has prepared us in the book of Joel 2:28–30: "And it shall come to pass afterward, That I will pour out My Spirit on all flesh; Your sons and your daughters shall prophesy, Your old men shall dream dreams, Your young men shall see visions. And also on My menservants and on My maidservants I will pour out My Spirit in those days." We must be encouraged to call upon Jesus, because He is the resurrection and life. He is sitting at the right hand of God as our advocate. He has all power over the angels, authorities, principalities, and dominions, and is Lord of the Sabbath; all things are made subject to Him.

CHAPTER 13

Praying to Know Him - The Ultimate Prayer

When we cannot let go of the things that we've lost, we tend to feel pain, sadness, or an emptiness inside. Sometimes, our pain could be the force to guide us towards another path. Somehow, we must remember that if we love God, it is written in His word that all things good and bad are working out for the good of those who love the Lord.

The different roads that we travel in life to discover meaning and purpose were divinely laid out for us by God so that we would desire to know Him. There is nothing that happens by accident or coincidence when He is revealing things to us through His word and mercies.

The Lord has a way of using the good and the bad things that happen to us for His glory. His plan is always in motion, because He desires to be included in our lives on a daily basis. We may not be able to comprehend what God is doing in our situation; sometimes we need to stop trying to put logic to the matter and hold on to believing that He knows all things and when we love Him we will turn to Him. He is our refuge; therefore, we must continue to believe in Him and give thanks and praise for everything that we go through.

Consequently, He will give us rest when our souls are weary. As we reflect upon the times when many of us should have been charged guilty for something we did wrong, but instead we were given mercy and grace. There have been times when we weren't always honest about some things, but we still received mercy. When we chose to go our own way instead of following the Holy Spirit's promptings, things still worked out in our favor. Let's face it: if God was not on our side, there's no telling where we'd end up.

We should never allow what we've gone through to hold us back from telling our testimony. The things that we're willing to share about the journey gives hope and strength to others and lets them know that they can make it through, too. The Lord has done a lot for us, and we're His witnesses to the world; it gives Him glory to know that we're grateful for everything that He does for our family and friends.

The fruit of our prayers has been effective, because He continues to show us love. So, it doesn't matter how wealthy, successful, influential, or beautiful we may become. He shows no partiality nor favoritism towards us. We are all flawed human beings and will never be able to live a perfect and spotless life. By having status and power, it still doesn't blind God's eyes, because He sees us for who we really are. But it is evident that we need each other's love, so we may experience how God feels about loving us unconditionally.

When we experience love, it helps us to grow into compassionate human beings. There are times when we may feel completely helpless, alone, and in need of someone to support us while we're going through a storm, an illness, event, or bereavement of a loved one. It does the soul well when we are connected to other people that care about us and are willing to pray and stand by our side. As believers, we know that there's a mighty God working behind the scenes in our lives, mending all of the pieces to the brokenness, sorrow, struggles, pain, and suffering.

Nevertheless, we are always moving along the path; we are guided by our beliefs, choices, and thoughts that we think. We seem to attract the kinds of people that we are alike the most. It's hard to see when our pride, ego, and stubbornness gets in the way of us achieving our goals, dreams, and our destiny, because we're not willing to accept constructive criticism that could very well turn our situations around or enlighten us.

Therefore, we put up walls and believe that we should have it all together, so no one knows just how much we need help and love. We are guarded about the things that we feel society looks down upon, and our hearts can become hardened when someone wants to genuinely help us.

We may feel that our family and friends will always be there for us, but somehow things just don't always turn out the way we planned it. People are always changing; they move away, die, become ill, separate, and meet new people, but life goes on.

We must have an open heart to receive the people that God sends to us, because they have something that we need and vice versa. We learn from being around different people, having new experiences, and having a forgiving heart. There is so much that the Lord wants to do through us, but we have to get out of the way. We cannot predict how God will show up in our lives, but it's likely He will use the people that we never would have imagined to help and bless us.

When we are ready to give up after putting our trust into people and the things that have failed us, our mind, thoughts, and emotions become bombarded with a plethora of lies and confusion. We must face it: we'll never be able to figure out everything, nor can we know God's will for our lives without seeking Him first through prayer and studying the word.

When our strength is gone and we're tired of doing things our way, are we ready to listen? No matter how difficult life may seem, at the end of each day God is always watching over us. He continues to nourish our souls by providing us food, shelter, and protection along with new mercies and grace. That's why it is important to pray to know Christ.

Many believers continue to seek exterior things, because they have not truly tasted how good the Lord is. As time goes on, we must learn that there's no value in accumulating material things, because it doesn't bring us closer to knowing who God is. God is Spirit and He is love; we need to seek being filled with the Holy Spirit and start praying and asking God for it.

The Holy Spirit is a part of the Triune God: God the Father, God the Son, and God the Holy Spirit. The Holy Spirit was sent by God when His Son, Jesus, ascended into Heaven after being resurrected from the grave. The Holy Spirit is sent to live inside of Christ's disciples, anyone who has accepted

Jesus Christ as their Lord and Savior and are following Him. The Holy Spirit is our teacher, counselor, and helper, and He gives us the power to live holy. Otherwise, we would not be able to refrain from living a life of sin.

We must evaluate our behavior by being honest with how we perceive God. We know that He's someone that we call upon to answer our prayers, but it cannot always be a one-sided relationship. The ultimate prayer that we should petition while living is praying to know Him. When our hearts remain focused on the exterior parts of our lives, we have no spiritual knowledge of who He is, nor His Son, Jesus Christ.

When we desire to know someone intimately, we have to sacrifice, putting in the time. We can learn so much about each other's feelings, strengths, and weaknesses. We even create a stronger bond when we share our ups and downs together. However, the most precious thing that matters about our relationships is knowing that we are unconditionally loved and knowing that we are mentally, emotionally, and spiritually willing to reciprocate it to the people we love.

As we learn to love unconditionally, we will understand how to love God and His Son, Jesus. He understands us, because God became flesh in Jesus while He walked the earth and He has feelings like we do. The time and effort that we put into pursuing human love, we need to sacrifice the same in pursuing to know who God is for ourselves; we need to remain faithful and steadfast in seeking a relationship with His Son, Jesus. He offered us His love before we even knew anything about who He was.

There was a penalty for our sins against God, and God was willing to accept the ultimate sacrifice of Jesus' blood for the atonement, redemption, and reconciliation. Mankind fell from grace into sin when Adam and Eve disobeyed God in the Garden of Eden. Sin separates us from having a close relationship with God, but when He sent His only begotten Son, Jesus, it reconciled us back to having a relationship with God.

The clock starts ticking towards eternity when we confess with our mouths that Jesus is Lord and believe in our hearts that God raised Him from the grave; we are saved. Romans 10:9–10 says, "That if you confess with your mouth the Lord Jesus and believe in your heart that God has raised Him from the dead, you will be saved. For with the heart one believes unto righteousness, and with the mouth confession is made unto salvation." We can put our hope and trust in serving Him as Lord of our lives, because we were purchased by His blood to be counted as His own. He removed the burden and guilt that sin had on us by restoring and adopting us into His Father's family.

However, we will never be free from sin until we are no longer residing in our physical bodies; when we sin and make mistakes and can't seem to get things right, we must repent, turn to Jesus, and ask for God's forgiveness. Therefore, that is why we are given the Holy Bible to read, study, and learn about Him, so we can learn for ourselves what pleases God and how we should relate to and obey Him.

We need to understand what Jesus did for us, so we can fathom how much He loves us. He took our beatings, went to hades, conquered death, and nailed all our sins with each strike of the hammer to the cross. He is the risen Savior our Lord; through the power of the Holy Spirit, we have been sealed to Christ in our past, present, and forever. He is waiting and listening to our prayers.

It is our choice and free will to believe what is written in the word of God. We are tested when we hear our family, friends, and non-believers speaking negatively about Christ and saying things such as, "Man wrote the Bible and it's a lie." We are going to always have skeptics everywhere we go; but remember, God is Spirit, and science cannot comprehend spiritual revelations to outsmart or compete with God. Some of these same people are dying without knowing that Christ is the risen Savior and He can save them from condemnation and eternal death if they would only repent and accept Jesus Christ as their Lord and Savior. There is no other God that promises what Christ has offered to all nations: the gift of salvation and eternal life. God's spirit is infinite; we must be wise to not lean on our own understanding but in all our ways trust in the Lord, and He will direct our paths.

Everyone has a right to their opinion; however, many are called, but few are chosen. Do you want to know Christ? Have you accepted Him? The day that you hear the knock at the door, please be careful to not ignore it. The word of God tells us in the book of Revelations 3:20, "Behold, I stand at the door and knock. If anyone hears My voice and opens the door, I will come in to him and dine with him, and he with Me. To him who overcomes I will grant to sit with Me on My throne, as I also overcame and sat down with My Father on His throne."

It is vital that every believer must continue to pray for a relationship in knowing God's Son, Jesus. When our love for Christ is genuine, we will no longer feel apart from Him; we are conscious of what violates it. We know who He is to us, our Savior; the cost of giving up His life for our sins; and His gift to us for Salvation and eternal life with Him and the Father. Through the word and Holy Spirit, we are connected to Jesus and are willing to abide with Him.

As we come to Christ through prayer and worship asking for grace and mercy, we need to open our hearts to the Lord Jesus and let Him search us. We must give it all to Him: the un-forgiveness, hatred, anger, drugs, lewdness, religious mind, gossip, envy, jealousy, greed, pride, witchcraft, or whatever sin that is hidden in our hearts. It doesn't matter what sin is holding us back from going deeper in God; we will not be able to continue to hide our sins in the closet while attending church every week and refusing to repent or be accountable for the sin that we know is against God's word. The world is watching us and is being impacted by how we live our lives.

In conclusion, we may feel that we've heard the message about Christ and have read the word enough, but we do not fully know who Jesus is until our searching leads us to having a personal relationship with Him and our hearts are resting and abiding in Him.

We need to become consciously aware of showing love to other Christians who chose to believe in a different doctrine than ours. The body of Christ is divided and impacted by the many doctrines of the Christian faith. If we are reading and studying the Holy Bible, there is no reason to follow any other doctrine than Christ. We can talk about the word in this way or that way or become so religious minded to the point that we miss the main point. Jesus is the only one that saves and in whom we should place our hope, faith, and honor.

We should turn our complete focus towards understanding the life of Jesus and His message of love and the great commission. When we truly get this part understood, we will attract others who are connected to Christ's love too.

Yet, we still remain divided because of the way that we behave towards each other. The royal law commands us to love our neighbor as ourselves (Romans 13:10). We lack showing the love of Christ, because we have not learned what it truly means to love and we have allowed our allegiance to our church doctrine to hold a place of honor in our lives by determining whether to evangelize, fellowship, and show Christ's love to people who do not go to our church, worship like we do, nor believe in our doctrine.

As we examine our lives, are we following the life of Christ? The word tells us in the book of John 14:7, "Jesus is the way, the truth, and the life." We need to pray, pray, pray for revelation when reading the scriptures. The Holy Spirit wants us to know what the Father is revealing in His word and wants us to be filled with truth and knowledge so that we can stop wavering back and forth in knowing who Jesus is.

Sometimes, we tend to feel comfortable in doing works because we're good at what we do; but without realizing it, our pride could be motivating us. We must remain cognizant that we cannot obtain righteousness through works nor salvation and that pride is a sin. If we get into a consecrated and quiet place with God during our day, the Holy Spirit will reveal many things to us. He is personal and wants to make His presence known to us.

When things get to us, we are at our most vulnerable state and need to be careful of what doors we open and be mindful that we are not as vigilant as we should be. We must guard our minds and hearts daily by being careful of the company we keep, the things we watch and listen to, and the words we speak by examining our actions and motives.

Please know that it's okay when people talk bad about us, because they may have found fault in us; when we repent, God's mercies are new every day, and His grace is sufficient. We all have fallen short because of our sins according to God. However, we can count ourselves blessed when God vindicates us, because we all will be judged individually for everything done in secret and in the light according to God's standards.

The closer we get in knowing God, we will no longer desire to keep holding on to the hurt from the past, nor looking back at the things we lost. Remember, while we're going through hurtful things, sometimes it's ordained by God to help prepare us to be used for His will. The way that He trains us to listen to Him may be painful, but we're going to become better servants when the time comes to be effective to others who may need our help and encouragement. So, we must not look at our problems and lives as a mistake, because God knows why He created everyone and the purpose to their lives.

When we accept what the Bible tells us about our true identity, we will no longer care about what man thinks or says about who we are. We will find peace and gain the freedom to become whom God wants us to be. The word of God tells us in 2 Corinthians 5:17, "Therefore, if anyone is in Christ, he is a new creation; old things have passed away, behold, all things have become new." The world can only see the outside, but Christ sees all and knows everything inside and out about everyone.

We are passing through this life, and we only have a short time here. If God doesn't say yes and answer all of our prayers or decide to heal us, we should never lose sight of knowing that we are saved by grace and given the gift of salvation through our faith in God. This gift of eternal life means more than any bliss that we could find or ask for, because knowing Jesus is the ultimate answer to all our prayers.

The Ultimate Prayer

Jesus, You are the ultimate prayer
I have life and victory through the power of your authority
Help me to witness that You are, Lord

Please draw me closer to the well where the rivers flow
The prayers of the righteous cry out to you
Lord, I am praying to know you more

I have purpose and my heart is renewed
The price for my life was predestined to be yours
My soul is connected through your love and mercy

I shall live to tell my story that I know you
You are called the resurrection and life
You are God and your presence alone completes me